Advance Praise for
Seeking Sanity

"*Seeking Sanity* brings together ancient wisdom and modern mental health in a practical guidebook that encourages us to discover the essential happiness that is already within us all. With honest stories, clear insights, and practical exercises, author Joseph DeNicholas gives us a map and tools to find wellbeing and live fully as we navigate these challenging times. I highly recommend this book."

—**Loch Kelly**, M.Div, LCSW,
Creator of Mindful Glimpses app

"Joe DeNicholas's practical approach to discovering our innate sanity offers a plethora of methods and practice techniques to align us with the best of ourselves. Reading the book feels like a coaching session, and Joe's unique analytical mind, combined with his therapeutic training and Buddhist studies, offers a fresh and original take on applied Buddhist psychology."

— **Melissa Moore**, PhD, Author of *The Diamonds Within Us*

"*Seeking Sanity* is both a philosophical and practical guide that encourages us to relax our obsession with external fixes and begin cultivating the inner qualities that create lasting peace. With relatable honesty and actionable exercises, Joe DeNicholas provides readers with the tools to confront themselves, change their habits, and live with greater clarity and resilience."

— **Fred Stone**, PhD, LCSW

"In *Seeking Sanity*, Joe DeNicholas offers a practical blueprint for staying grounded, clear-headed, and connected to what truly matters, even when the world around us seems to have gone stark raving mad. A timely, essential read for navigating today's chaos."

— **Gregg Spiridellis**, Founder of JibJab & StoryBots

SEEKING SANITY

HOW TO CULTIVATE PEACE, HAPPINESS, AND WELLBEING IN A WORLD GONE MAD

JOSEPH DeNICHOLAS MBA, LCSW

modern wisdom
PRESS

Modern Wisdom Press
Crestone, Colorado, USA
www.ModernWisdomPress.com

Copyright © Joseph DeNicholas MBA, LCSW, 2025

All rights reserved. No part of this publication may be reproduced or transmitted in any form or by any means, mechanical or electronic, including photocopying or recording, or by any information storage and retrieval system, or transmitted by email, without permission in writing from the author. Reviewers may quote brief passages in reviews.

Disclaimer: To protect the privacy of certain individuals, some names and identifying details have been changed. Neither the author nor the publisher assumes any responsibility for errors, omissions, or contrary interpretations of the subject matter within.

Medical Disclaimer: The content in this book is not intended to be a substitute for professional medical advice, diagnosis, or treatment. Always seek the advice of your physician or other qualified health provider for questions you may have regarding a health concern or medical diagnosis.

Published 2025

ISBNs: 978-1-951692-53-7 (paperback)
 978-1-951692-54-4 (eBook)

Cover design by Karen Sperry
Back cover and author page photos courtesy of Anna DeNicholas

*I dedicate this effort to
all my Buddhist teachers, mentors,
and spiritual friends.
Thank you for plucking me from
the ocean of suffering.
I hope I've made all of you proud.*

OM MANI PADME HUNG HRI

TABLE OF CONTENTS

Foreword 9
Introduction (Please don't skip) 13

Chapter 0: Learning to Calm Down 23

PART 1: UNDERSTANDING WHAT HAPPENED TO YOU

Chapter 1:   Assessing Flawed Goals and
Ineffective Strategies 33
Chapter 2:   Discovering Your Great Self 61

PART 2: DEVELOPING A SOLUTION

Chapter 3:   Recognizing the Immaculate Being
That You Are 91
Chapter 4:   Learning How to Change 115

PART 3: THE PRACTICES

Chapter 5:   Cultivating Joyful Diligence 141
Chapter 6:   Learning How to Be 157
Chapter 7:   Mastering Your Emotions 181
Chapter 8:   Knowing Thy (Small) Self 195
Chapter 9:   Setting Intentions and Nurturing Reflection 207
Chapter 10: Checking and Renewing 219

Chapter 11: Living Sanely in an Insane World 225

Afterword: The Most Beautiful Platitude 235
Appendix I: Maladaptive Schemas 239
Appendix II: Maladaptive Schema Modes 245
Appendix III: Defense Mechanisms 249
Glossary 257
Endnotes 263
Additional Resources 266
In Gratitude 267
About The Author 271

FOREWORD

Modern culture offers us an endless stream of images promoting happiness. It implies that we're inadequate, but we could be improved by a product we can buy. It relentlessly tells us that we'll be happy if we go on this diet, drive a fancier car, acquire the newest smartphone, or get fresher breath and a whiter smile.

Maybe we believe, based on our family or societal expectations, that we must be married, have kids, own a house, and so on to really feel happy. Or perhaps we envision ourselves in a successful career that will bring money and prominence, and we think *that* will lead to happiness. Maybe we want to throw ourselves into endless rounds of entertainment, living in a perpetual party like a pop star, in one pleasurable experience after the next.

But what if we're still unhappy, even after we've achieved one of these circumstances where we imagine happiness will be our reward…what then?

There's something meaningful and profound about this level of unhappiness that doesn't fit into our image of a good life. There's value to this suffering because it's our intelligence starting to percolate and question how we're living our lives. It's telling us we have something we vitally need to learn.

Something you can learn from the wisdom within these pages.

The truth is, no amount of entertainment, money, possessions, or drugs dispels our internal agitation once and for all. All our solutions have been external, while the problem of unhappiness begins within us. We've looked for something outside ourselves to save us, while we've never really looked carefully at who we are, at our own mind, and really tried to understand and relate to it.

We were never taught how. For all its lavish material sophistication, our society fails to train us in the most fundamental ways of working with our own minds. But *Seeking Sanity* addresses this very issue.

This book will help you understand how you might become confused, unhappy, and out of sorts in your life and provide you with immediate ways to address and come to terms with these issues.

As the author emphasizes, however, when it comes to authentically learning about your mind, purely reading books and picking up some theory will not resolve the mind's core distress. If you want to genuinely understand how your mind works, you must look within yourself, feel what you feel, and face whatever you must face. In this way, you'll come to true, lived, experiential knowledge.

I met author Joseph DeNicholas many years ago when he came to volunteer at my organization, Mindfulness Peace Project. We teach meditation and the spiritual path to prison inmates and military veterans. He worked as an instructor in our study courses, and we had many discussions about the issues that crop up when teaching people how to work with their minds and develop themselves spiritually.

Mr. DeNicholas has studied extensively enough to earn degrees in electrical engineering, business, and clinical social work. He faced his own need to unravel his personal confusion with his customary energy and sharp focus, developing himself through cultivating meditative knowledge and experience. He has raised a family, gone back to school to become a therapist, and developed a way to present his understanding to others that genuinely helps them find their footing and navigate their way.

You can actively avoid your inner life out of fear of what you might find. But this approach only ties you in knots, as you wonder why you don't feel happy or free.

There's unavoidable and very personal work involved to find lasting happiness. The good news is, what you don't necessarily know—and usually no one teaches you—is that *there's nothing essentially wrong with your mind*. There IS something wrong with how you *habitually relate* to your thoughts, emotions, and perceptions. This forms the basis of *Seeking Sanity*'s message. Enormous delusion and conflict arise from blindly grasping at and fixating on thoughts and mental projections. It distorts our perception of the world and encourages struggle and conflict with those around us.

But as the author explains, the mind itself, in its original essence, exists as an unconditional awareness that sees clearly and open-heartedly through our mental deceptions.

This is the sanity we've needed all along. Lacking this connection, we become disturbed as individuals and dissonant as a society. You can scavenge the whole world, overturning every rock, trying to find what you've always had inside. Most of us just need the courage and gumption to look for it there.

Let *Seeking Sanity* be your trusted companion on the journey of looking within and befriending your mind. The straight talk and insight shared by Mr. DeNicholas result from a life of learning and applied experience. This book offers, concisely, both the point of view necessary to understand your innate happiness and the tools to practically bring it about in your daily experience. You might uncover a joy and sanity you didn't know you had.

Gary Allen
Co-Executive Director
Mindfulness Peace Project

INTRODUCTION

(PLEASE DON'T SKIP)

> The mind makes for a good and useful servant, but a very poor master.
>
> — UNKNOWN

In 2004, I accepted a new job designing integrated circuit chips (the tiny bits of silicon that run almost everything today). I wanted my first chip to be perfect, not only because it was my first project at this company, but also because I had long staked my self-worth on scholastic and professional achievement. After many months of arduous design work, and a few more anxious months waiting for the prototype to be manufactured, it came time for the most critical test. This particular test was the electrical engineering equivalent of taking a baseball bat to a carton of eggs. My hands shook a little as I attached the electrodes that would deliver the intended punch.

Pow! Sparks flew into the air, and a wisp of smoke ascended as the chip gave up the ghost.

To say that my heart sank would be the understatement of the century. As irrational as I may have been in that moment, I truly believed my future was riding on this chip. *This can't be happening,*

I thought. I double-checked my setup, replaced the damaged device, and tried again.

Bang! Sparks once again confirmed the horrifying conclusion: My design contained a fatal flaw—a bug.

Then I experienced my first-ever panic attack. My hands shook uncontrollably, my throat tightened, my breath quickened. I experienced hot flashes as my mind spun. The world seemed surreal. Time stood still like I was in a horror movie.

Reality sank in as paranoia hijacked my mind, filling it with racing, discursive, afflicted thoughts without a moment's respite. It wasn't long before I had trouble sleeping, collapsing out of exhaustion around 11:00 PM and waking up somewhere around 2:00 AM, full of anxious energy. Within days, I noticed I was hardly hungry anymore, given that constant worry and sadness can do a real number on the appetite. I regularly had dry heaves before work. I was descending into darkness without a brake lever.

Before you follow me too far down the rabbit hole of suffering, I want you to know that this horror story shifts into a beautiful one of healing and personal transformation. I'm not merely advertising a good Hollywood ending; I wholeheartedly believe that everyone is capable of such transformation when empowered with knowledge and the appropriate tools. So there's no need for despair or disheartenment. I'm sure you've had plenty of both already.

But before I get to the happy ending, I need to talk about what happened to us—how we ended up in this mess in the first place.

Mental illness and emotional instability are increasingly running over us in more ways than we can count. A USA Today/Suffolk University poll found that 9 out of 10 registered voters believe there's a "mental health crisis" in the nation.[1] Think about that—9 out of 10 Americans can't agree that the Earth is round,[2] yet nearly all of us agree that we've got a severe problem on our hands when it comes to our mental and emotional wellbeing.

Clinical levels of mental illness and addiction aren't the only things plaguing our society on the mental health front. There is a large portion of the population that I refer to as "not yet clinical, but not currently well." Sadly, many minds considered healthy by today's (insurance-based) standards are locked up in incessant, self-absorbed, judgmental, discursive chatter…and that's when they aren't being distracted by work, gossip, television, podcasts, gambling, social media, exercise, news, porn, drugs, alcohol, and myriad other avoidance mechanisms. Maybe this isn't clinical unwellness, but it surely isn't a picture of health either. So many people's lives have become devoid of meaning and purpose.

You may strive to be healthier but find that, more often than not, your desire for wellbeing is no match for your self-defeating, destructive habit patterns.

Unhealthy individuals form unhealthy communities. Self-absorption and conflict are exploding as social technologies pour jet fuel onto our fears, bringing the worst parts of ourselves into contact with the worst parts of others. Discourse is breaking down as we sort ourselves into tribal bubbles of like-minded people. A society is fundamentally a collection of individuals, and unfortunately, the overwhelming majority of individuals are doing little to nothing to address their own neuroses and mental illnesses.

Polish poet and aphorist Stanislaw Jerzy Lec described the situation perfectly: "No snowflake in an avalanche ever feels responsible." The point is to stop judging others as being the problem. If there is a problem, the thing you refer to as "me" is it, and it's a problem *you* have to work on, because no one else can. But that doesn't mean you must work on it alone, which is why I wrote this book.

EXPLORING MENTAL HEALTHCARE'S SHORTCOMINGS

Back to the horror-movie-turned-redemption story. I hadn't slept more than a couple hours or eaten a complete meal in a few weeks. This was about enough for my sister Sandy, who flew from Chicago to Phoenix and promptly dragged me to a psychiatrist. The doctor prescribed Zyprexa, an antipsychotic medication that would force me to sleep and eat. Over the next month, as sleep and nutrition returned, my mind "recovered" to a kind of pathetic homeostasis that included near-constant anxiety and depression.

It was around this time that I embarked on a numbed-out, heavily sedated, decade-long foray into pharmaceuticals. A second psychiatrist assured me that none of this was my fault because my brain—analogous to the pancreas of a person with diabetes—was exhibiting imbalances of essential neurotransmitters like serotonin and norepinephrine. I would be on these pills, he asserted, for the rest of my life.

Thankfully, I wasn't buying it. If I had a neurotransmitter deficiency, what was causing it? Did the chemical imbalances cause the mental states, or did the mental states cause the imbalances? It all seemed rather unscientific.

Don't get me wrong. I respect psychiatrists; they have helped me and millions of others. It's not an exaggeration to say they may have saved my life, and psychotropic medications certainly have their place in mental health treatment. However, in many cases, it often does people a disservice to convince them that little else can be done. Never once did either psychiatrist say, "Your problem is you, so you need to get to work" or anything close to it.

And they were simply wrong, because I haven't been on medication for years, so where's my "brain diabetes" now?

MERGING EAST AND WEST TO FIND WELLBEING

Because I find interest, beauty, and awe in the world, I've always been a voracious consumer of information. As a kid, I even read the entire encyclopedia—mostly while sitting on the toilet, as my mother loves to point out. So I began reading what I could find about the problem of human happiness and suffering. I headed to Barnes & Noble (a step up from the bathroom), which had a table of recent bestsellers at the front of the store. Prominently displayed in the middle of the table was the book *Happiness* by Matthieu Ricard.[3] It was a game-changer.

As gentle as the book is, one thing became apparent within hours: *My entire life had been a fraudulent enterprise that gave me little chance of achieving lasting peace, happiness, and fulfillment.* As a Midwestern, red-blooded American male, I was trained to believe that once I forced all the puzzle pieces into place—career, finances, spouse, children, house, car, entertainment—I would plant the flag on the hill of peace and happiness forever.

Silly me. Nothing could be further from the truth, because peace, happiness, and fulfillment are not based on an external set of circumstances forced into existence through great effort and sacrifice and held there. *They are internal conditions requiring cultivation.*

It wasn't a coincidence that Matthieu Ricard was a PhD biologist turned Buddhist monk. Buddhism is the world-class gem that offers an understanding of the mind, the self, reality, and factors and methods that lead to the arising of widely desired positive mental states and their associated virtues and outcomes. I'm not alone in this assertion, as this claim is now being espoused by many Western, non-Buddhist scientists and philosophers.[4, 5, 6, 7] Referring to the instructions provided to him by one of his Buddhist teachers, ardent atheist and learned philosopher and neuroscientist Sam Harris stated, "This instruction was, without question, the most important thing I have ever been explicitly taught by another human being. It has given me a way to escape the usual tides of psychological suffering—fear, anger, shame—in an instant."[8]

Thus in 2008, I enrolled in classes in Buddhist psychology and metaphysics—a body of knowledge so vast and deep that finding the bottom of it is impossible. I've studied it continuously ever since and enjoyed the good fortune to be trained in meditation by some of the world's top minds. These efforts complement my more traditional education in engineering, business, and clinical social work (therapy).

If I have a message for the world, it is this: We're failing a test we've been given the answers to, people! It's high time to put a stop to this madness. That's the purpose of this book.

HOW TO USE THIS BOOK

My MBA taught me that if you've failed to achieve a particular outcome, it's because you didn't understand your true goals, your strategies were flawed, or you stumbled in the execution of your strategies. Accordingly, this book is broken into three sections.

Part 1 covers how and why these failings occur.

- Chapter 0 provides exercises you can use to feel better right away, since I suspect that's why you're here.

- Chapter 1 reviews definitions of peace, happiness, and overall wellbeing to help you clarify what your true aims are. Then you'll explore a few of the dominant (but failed) strategies you may have used for achieving them.

The chapters in Part 2 provide background on how your brain works and how habits form so you can learn to alter both.

- Chapter 2 introduces models of the brain. Here you'll learn about changing from a small self to a Great Self perspective and how that leads to a more stable version of yourself.

- Chapter 3 discusses the wonderful traits or characteristics of the Great Self that will be the basis for your (new) life.

- Chapter 4 teaches you how humans effect change in their lives to ensure you proceed with confidence. I'll share two paths forward, which you will use as you work through the practices in the remaining chapters.

Part 3 contains practices you can use to achieve the emotional stability you desire.

- Chapters 5 through 10 teach you practices to implement throughout your day to feel better, build confidence in your path toward growth and wellbeing, and keep everyday calamities from derailing you.

> Of course, you don't have to stop there. In addition to the content in this book, you can access a variety of additional resources to deepen inner peace and wellbeing on my website at www.UnbreakableInc.com. While you're there, you can also sign up for one of my workshops or retreats if you'd prefer to learn and practice together, get your questions answered, and maybe even meet like-minded people.

There's a global peace, happiness, and wellbeing movement occurring, and I don't want you to miss it. This journey isn't about tweaking a few habits or adding another self-help hack to your routine. It's about transformation—a shift in how you think about, conduct yourself within, and mentally and emotionally interact with the chaos of modern life.

This book challenges you to question fundamental assumptions about who you are, what peace and happiness truly mean, and how to achieve mental and emotional wellbeing. The topics are deep, and several will likely be entirely new and even a bit radical to you, so please don't be surprised if this isn't a quick weekend read. Most importantly, please have no fear: *Nothing I say in this book will require you to change your chosen faith path, and I would prefer that you not do so.*

Some of what this book covers will be provocative; that's one of the reasons I'm writing it. Out of love and from a place of deep compassion, I'm going to wake you from your slumber and get the gorilla that is your mind off the couch. I tried to make this a little entertaining, but modern human society is very effective at separating us from our true nature, so to move forward, you will have to cut through the significant confusion that this causes.

Society conditions us to believe that working, achieving, consuming, and distracting our way to an empty, self-absorbed happiness that is too devoid of meaning, purpose, and connection will work out. No wonder we're so frustrated and exhausted. No wonder our societal structures are being ripped apart, as various factions attempt to exert control over each other under the belief that their version of reality is "right." Enough already!

CHAPTER 0

LEARNING TO CALM DOWN

Chapter 0? Yes, electrical engineers like myself typically start counting at zero, but that's not the reason for the title. It's more because I want to help you set up a base of operations so you can start calming down and feeling better immediately, and I know you're capable of it. I also want your mind to be calm and pliable—ready to learn and grow while (hopefully!) enjoying the process I've outlined for you.

Two assumptions form the basis of all practices in this book.

- Emotions are combinations of mental and physical events.
- There's a place in your mind that's already peaceful and happy but is currently too often obscured.

The next section looks into each of these assumptions before you get to the exercises to help you feel better.

UNDERSTANDING YOUR EMOTIONS

Emotions are combinations of mental and physical phenomena, so to feel better, you need to address both domains. For example, worry often presents as incessant, futuristic thinking (mental phenomena) and tension in various muscles, including the digestive tract (physical phenomena). Either domain can kick off the emoting process.

To experience firsthand how thoughts activate bodily sensations, think about all the reasons you last became angry, and notice what happens in your body. In turn, physical sensations activate thoughts, as your left brain tries to figure out why the body has been activated and make sense of it. Thus thoughts can generate physical sensations, and physical sensations can generate thoughts. You get stuck in mini emotional loops all day, every day, which is why you love your distractions—they're currently your only means of escape. Consequently, working with emotions means working skillfully with your body *and* mind.

FINDING YOUR MIND'S PEACEFUL PLACE

There is a place in your mind that is peaceful no matter what's going on at any moment. It's actually the base, or *natural*, state of your mind. All thinking, interpreting, mental storytelling, and emotional reactivity are *perturbations* or disturbances of this state. The problem is that your mind has been incessantly disturbing itself for so long that you've (incorrectly) come to believe that neurotic rumination is the base state of your mind. The mind improves at whatever it does, which is why you practice everything from golf to mathematics. This automatic learning process is a blessing and a curse.

To understand why it is difficult to experience peace of mind, imagine how peaceful you would be with someone poking, questioning, or criticizing you constantly! This is what your mind has been doing to itself for a very long time—possibly your whole life. That's the curse. The blessing arises when you learn to take control of the habituation process and intentionally cultivate peace and stability. The Tibetan word for meditation is *gom* (rhymes with comb), which literally means "to become familiar with." Thus your mission is to become increasingly and intimately familiar with this stable place and all it has to offer.

USING THE 4–7–8 BREATHING TECHNIQUE TO STOP STRESS

I tell my clients that mental patterns take time to develop, as do the practices required to alter those patterns. Furthermore, no practice is equally effective for every kind of mind. So if a technique works for you, great! If, after a reasonable effort, a practice isn't doing much for you, just let it go. This particular practice is the first one I give to every client. Almost all of them find it valuable to give themselves permission to snap out of mindless rumination, assess how they are really feeling, and relax the body and mind. In this exercise, you begin by taking the time to assess your current state and then calm your body and mind with a couple of simple techniques.

1. **Check in.** Take a moment to assess the state of your body and mind right now. Simply close your eyes and scan your body, noting any sensations that are present. Then check on your state of mind. Use one word to describe what you find.

2. **Calm your body through muscle relaxation.** If your body scan found muscle tension, tense each of those muscles fully for a few seconds and then allow it to relax. Alternatively, massage a tense area while breathing into it. Be sure to check your shoulders, face, and belly since these are some of tension's favorite hangout spots. Lastly, tense up all your muscles at once—even the muscles in your face—for a few seconds, then relax completely. (And be sure to crack a smile at how silly you just looked.)

3. **Calm your body with the 4–7–8 breath.** Inhale *through your nose* for four seconds, hold your breath for seven seconds, exhale *through pursed lips* (like you're blowing out a candle) for eight seconds, and *note how you feel at the end* (key point). That's it.

   If you have difficulty slowing the out breath down that much, try extending it for 10 seconds or even longer a few times, until you become familiar with what it's like to slow down.

Try a couple rounds of this technique now, mentally noting how your mind and body feel after each one. Maybe you detect a calming effect, and maybe you don't. Whatever you experience is okay!

Breathing techniques are scientifically proven to be effective[9] at calming the body and mind, though we didn't need EEG or fMRI scans to tell us that. This particular sequence is effective because it engages the parasympathetic nervous system, which calms you down when you're activated.

SNAPPING INTO RADICAL ACCEPTANCE

One theory of suffering suggests that it arises due to resistance to the immediate experience. It's helpful to distinguish between *what's happening* and *your relationship to what's happening*. Suffering results from your relationship—one based in fear, aversion, or even hatred—to painful, unpleasant experiences.

For this exercise, I want you to truly *know* that your mind completely controls its relationship to the present moment. I further want you to accept as fact that your mind can pivot to a more positive relationship in an instant. Now follow the sequence.

1. Define your current state of mind as identified in Step 1 of the previous exercise.

2. Reflect on the fact that your state of mind is inherently unstable and doesn't last. While this fact can be unsettling, it also provides the requisite space for a new state to arise. In other words, the impermanence of mental and emotional states provides space for new possibilities.

3. Fully feel whatever your state of mind is and say to yourself "This is my truth—for now—a starting point on my journey to happiness."

4. If your current state of mind is negative, ask yourself *why* you find it so unacceptable. Tag "So what? Who said…?" onto the end of every answer your mind produces. Develop whatever "who said" phrases you think will work for you.

Here's an example sequence:

> "My current state of mind, depression, is unacceptable because it's horribly unpleasant."
>
> *So what? Who said life wasn't going to be unpleasant sometimes?*
>
> "But I don't like it."
>
> *So what? Who said you were going to like everything?*
>
> "But I'm afraid I will be like this forever."
>
> *So what? Who said you would never be afraid in life?*
>
> Besides, you have no idea what's coming for you, so just cut it with all the prognosticating. Ask yourself if you're willing to stop fighting against reality and just be whatever, wherever, and whenever you are—right now.

5. Now snap your fingers, and in so doing, snap your mind into mindful awareness of the present moment, and drop all resistance whatsoever to your direct experience. Becoming hyper-mindful implies concentrating exclusively on what you see, hear, and feel. Completely surrender to this moment, and most importantly, feel what it's like to do so. Whatever you are, for now, you are—so BE IT. I don't need to tell you how to drop all resistance any more than I would need to tell you how to stop talking or walking. You just stop.

6. Now when you're ready—SNAP! Notice any shift in your experience.

These exercises are designed to teach you that you are not a helpless victim. If you commit some time to work with your mind and body throughout the day, you *will* feel better. These techniques require only a few seconds each, and no one in your scintillating employee communications meeting or at your in-laws' Thanksgiving dinner needs to know you're using them.

CHAPTER HIGHLIGHTS

In this chapter, you learned some techniques for quieting your mind. If one or more of these generated some shifts for you, great—if not, keep trying. Most of my clients need some practice with these exercises before they feel the full benefits. If they didn't work for you (yet), at least you've had a couple of moments of being present in your life, which is immensely beneficial in and of itself.

Key Insights

- You are not at the mercy of your mind or emotions.

- You can use intentional muscle relaxation and the 4-7-8 breath to calm your body and mind down.

- Snapping into radical acceptance—a total surrender to the now—can help you instantly slow your mind down when it is spinning.

It may sound obvious, but being a more peaceful and happy person entails spending more time every day in a peaceful and happy state. In that spirit, I'll refer back to these techniques throughout the book, reminding you to be kind and compassionate to yourself by slowing down, becoming present, taking a breath, and reminding yourself that you're sane. With practice, you'll become an expert in this sanity and be able to maintain it, even when life becomes a four-alarm dumpster fire and no one else in the space could possibly make such a radical claim.

Your time has come. Welcome to basic sanity. I'm so glad you're here.

Now that you've learned techniques to calm yourself, please move on to Chapter 1, which provides you with information to help you understand why peace and happiness have remained elusive and home in on what you really want in life. After all, you can only achieve your goals once you have soundly defined them.

PART 1

UNDERSTANDING WHAT HAPPENED TO YOU

CHAPTER 1

ASSESSING FLAWED GOALS AND INEFFECTIVE STRATEGIES

> In the pursuit of happiness, many people fail to find joy.
>
> — VIKTOR E. FRANKL

This much is obvious: Despite all of society's myriad advances in science, technology, and medicine—peace, happiness, and overall wellbeing remain elusive. Wasn't that the point of all those advances—to be happy and well? This chapter quickly and systematically assesses the situation to help you figure out what went wrong, dismantle it, and then fix it. Though the process should be fairly straightforward, it may also be a bit unpleasant. So take a deep breath (maybe one of those 4–7–8 breaths you just learned) and prepare to rip the Band-Aid off.

As I mentioned in the Introduction (which I know you didn't dare skip), my MBA taught me that failure to achieve a particular result occurs due to at least one of three reasons:

- You were confused about what you really wanted—the goals.

- You were confused about how to go about achieving your goals—the strategies.

- You failed to execute your strategies properly—the tactics.

Modern Western life presents you with countless strategies and tactics to achieve your goals. Most people assume these will be effective because they are the status quo, so there's no need to question them. But when no combination of the tried-and-true methods appears to work, no matter how well executed, the issues run deeper than mere tactics. This is a primary reason you've likely ended up frustrated and exhausted: You changed tactics or worked even harder by doubling down on the tactics you already employed, yet the desired outcomes remained elusive.

FORMING A NEW UNDERSTANDING OF HAPPINESS AND PEACE OF MIND

When I ask clients what they want in life, they typically say they want happiness, peace of mind, or both. But when I ask them to define those terms, they either say they don't know or say something like happiness is a *state* of mind resulting from the *presence* of the *desirable*, and peace of mind is a *state* of mind resulting from the *absence* of the *undesirable*. In other words, they believe they are happy when they get what they want and are peaceful when nothing bothers them.

Clients also report an important caveat: While they may experience *moments* of happiness and peace of mind, what they've strug-

Assessing Flawed Goals and Ineffective Strategies

gled to achieve is the *stability* of these states. To arrive at more specific goal definitions, you must first look at the most basic states of mind, namely pleasure and pain, *states* that result from the positive or negative subjective (specific to you, the subject) appraisal of a particular moment, respectively. It is important to note that pleasure and pain relate directly to what's happening in that moment—the circumstances.

For a more detailed explanation of these definitions and how I arrived at them, refer to the Glossary in the back of the book. For now, let's keep this straightforward. The key element is that pleasure and pain are subjective appraisals of what's happening at any given moment.

Now most people maintain that pleasure = happiness and pain = suffering (the opposite of peace of mind). Thus most people describe themselves as "happy" if they can string together significantly more pleasurable experiences than painful ones, and they suffer when they can't. It doesn't substantially matter if you're an unemployed, involuntarily celibate gamer living in your parents' basement or a highly esteemed professor who is happily married with three kids. Everyone is trying to maximize mental and physical states to match their desires in the context of their perceived capabilities and circumstances.

Using substitution (sorry, there's the nerd in me), the modified understanding of happiness and peace of mind can be defined as follows: Happiness is a state

> **GET THIS!**
>
> Most people believe happiness and peace of mind result from particular circumstances that must be forced into creation and held in place.

of mind resulting from the *presence* of circumstances *you* find pleasurable, and peace of mind is state of mind resulting from the *absence* of circumstances *you* find painful.

These modified definitions of happiness and peace of mind are the goals of modern life. Now that they are clearly defined, I'll briefly outline the top three (flawed) strategies people use to achieve happiness and peace of mind, and the fundamental problems that result from each strategy.

FLAWED STRATEGY #1: INCESSANT CIRCUMSTANCE MANAGEMENT

If happiness and peace of mind depend on circumstances, and you want them to remain stable, then the primary strategy for achieving them is obvious: You must *constantly manage the circumstances of your life*. Through tremendous and incessant effort, you are to force pleasurable circumstances into existence, hold them there indefinitely, and do whatever is required to avoid painful circumstances, both now and in the future. Circumstance management is what all the busy bees in the jar are doing. Investing aggressively in this strategy may consume your entire life, leaving only this activity and whatever distractions you use to avoid acknowledging that it isn't working well enough. Let's explore some of the reasons such a strategy is doomed to fail.

- **Happiness and peace of mind are internal conditions that already exist.** Happiness and peace of mind are internal, not external. Managing internal circumstances through external means is inherently problematic because it ignores this root point of confusion.

For example, you've likely heard the phrase "Beauty is in the eye of the beholder," but there's much more to this statement than initially meets the eye. Say someone already has a perfectly working coffee mug, so they don't *need* another. But then they see mine and like it better than theirs. Their next question will inevitably be "Where'd you get that?"

Now not everyone agrees that this is a desirable mug, which implies that the "goodness" of the object originates within the *subject*, but they don't know that. They mistakenly believe the goodness resides in the *object*, so they pull it into their territory to keep experiencing its goodness—the goodness they projected onto the external object from within themselves.

In other words, they crave the object because they aren't able to experience that internal goodness directly, so they attempt to experience it *by proxy* of the external. This mistake is why you're always so deeply engaged in the "pursuit of happiness," a fundamental right enshrined in the Declaration of Independence. I hate to be the bearer of bad news (not really; I am a therapist, after all), but this is the inherent problem with the circumstance management strategy: As long as you're in pursuit of something, *you don't have it*. The monumental irony is that you *do* have it; you just *don't know* you have it. Oops.

- **Impermanence is a fact of life.** External circumstances are inherently impermanent and, therefore, constantly changing. Every engineer will tell you that as soon as you put something together, entropy is working tirelessly to take it apart. Everything you own is future junk. Money comes and goes. (Trust me on that one.) Every favorable situation will eventually end, because everything created disintegrates. This inevitability implies that the circumstance management strategy runs counter to a fundamental fact of reality—impermanence—and that's a problem. Practically speaking, this means that the stress and exertion required to force the circumstances to your liking will be replaced with the stress and exertion required to try and hold them there while they do nothing but change. This is a fool's errand that only ends in disappointment!

> **GET THIS!**
> Everything is constantly changing, so attempting to incessantly control reality is an inherently exhausting, frustrating, and stressful approach to life.

Internal circumstances, including your desires, are also in a constant state of change. If you don't believe me, listen to your favorite song a few thousand times. (Wait, don't do that—you'll end up hating your favorite song.) That this happens to us suggests that humans are insatiable; the pleasure you achieve and pains you avoid can never fully satisfy you. The satisfaction of a craving only leads to more craving, like an itch that only gets worse from scratching, leading to a life of perpetual dissatisfaction.

This feedback loop is how addiction gets rolling. What every addict craves most is a moment without craving. Dissatisfaction directly results from the brain's inherent inability to achieve satiety. Nagarjuna, an important Buddhist philosopher from the second century, famously said, "Better to not have the itch than the pleasure of scratching."

- **You lack adequate control of circumstances.** External circumstances are far more out of control than you need for circumstance management to be effective. Sure, you can and should work hard and make lots of money, but that still won't give you what you need and want with any guarantee of stability. If such a strategy were effective, wealthy and powerful people would always be happy and peaceful, which is neither what we observe nor what they report. Why? Because they've achieved positive but unstable *states* but not positive and stable *traits*.

  No matter who you are or what you achieve, you can't control employees, friends or family members, competitors, politics, economies, pandemics, technological developments, the weather, natural disasters, or unnatural disasters. The list could go on forever. Regardless of how much money you have, you can't make people love you, nor can you stop yourself or those you love from aging, getting ill, and dying.

  This lack of adequate control points directly at another inherent flaw in the strategy: Relying on out-of-control external circumstances for wellbeing leads to one of the most crippling conditions crushing society today—hyper-vigilance, also known as *anxiety*.

Internal circumstances are also out of control, as anyone who has meditated for more than a few seconds will report. A professor in therapy school said we should never use the word *crazy*. I raised my hand. "Uhhhh, have you ever watched your brain operate for an hour straight in meditation? That thing is full-on nuts!"

> **GET THIS!**
> Relying on control of ever-changing situations full of unpredictable people automatically results in anxiety.

The thing is, we're all a little unhinged, but this is only a problem if you fail to maintain a healthy perspective about it, which entails lightening up quite a bit. I'm going to show you how to view and work with your particular brand of nuttiness so it doesn't affect you.

- **Circumstance management is expensive.** Pleasure-seeking and pain avoidance involve consumption, and lots of it. Consumption is costly, not only to ourselves but also to the planet and other animals who live here. Pleasure-seeking and pain avoidance are also costly in terms of the traditional way we think about cost—monetarily. And if you're going to *spend* lots of money, you need to *make* lots of money. So you'll need a high-paying job that takes a lot of time, which is yet another massive expense. This cycle creates the conditions for stress.

I hope you can see at this point that basing your wellbeing on the pursuit of pleasure and avoidance of pain is a dead end. It can't possibly work out long-term. The "pleasure = happiness, pain = suffering" paradigm leads you to outsource your wellbeing to an increasingly unreliable world full of unreliable people you can't control nearly enough and turns you into a dopamine addict. This outsourcing also causes you to wake up every day and ask the world "What kind of day do I get to have?"

Tell me what you rely on, and I'll tell you why your peace and happiness are so unstable.

As a funny example, I had a client struggling with their teenage children. I said I wanted them to try saying the following phrase without even cracking a smile: "I'm relying on American teenagers for my happiness and peace of mind." I'm sure you'll be shocked to learn they couldn't do it but instead laughed hysterically at the statement's ridiculousness.

FLAWED STRATEGY #2: ENGAGING IN AGGRESSIVE INDIVIDUALISM AND SELF-ABSORPTION

Doubling down on individualism and self-absorption is the most common reaction to the failure of circumstance management to achieve stable peace, happiness, and overall wellbeing. Since happiness and peace of mind (as defined) depend on *you* getting *your* way, maybe you just need to care more about yourself and what *you* want.

I discuss self-absorption more deeply in Chapter 2, but for now it's important to determine whether this thought pattern is present in your mind. If it would help to make that real for you, check in again on your ruminating mind and see who is playing the role of protagonist or antagonist (or possibly both) in the little soap opera.

Here are two of the most common problems you will encounter if you adopt this strategy.

Self-absorption *is* suffering. One of my Buddhist teachers, Ajahn Brahmavamso, defined suffering as "the egoic demand that reality be different than it is." Using this as our working definition of suffering, an immutable law of the universe emerges: As self-absorption and all its egoic demands increase, so will suffering. You've never suffered for any other reason, and there's no escape from this basic fact of reality. Anxiety and depression are diseases of self-absorption, as are most mental afflictions. Self-absorption *seems* like the right move, but it isn't.

As an example, here's a relatively typical Monday night in the DeNicholas household.

> *Me:* Can you take your sister to school in the morning?
>
> *Anna (17 years old):* No, my first period isn't until ten, so there's no way I'm getting up at seven.
>
> *Me:* Many people sacrifice for you, but you don't want to carry your fair share of the load. And as I've said a million times, self-absorption is the root of all suffering, so try to get the focus off you. Okay?
>
> *Anna:* You say that, but it makes no sense! Getting out of bed two hours early will *definitely* make me suffer, and staying in bed will make me happy. I might remind you that I'm not planning on having kids for a reason!

Assessing Flawed Goals and Ineffective Strategies

Me: Right. Your version of happiness seems to be you getting your way, and you suffer whenever you don't. Thanks for making my point for me. I love you and hope you understand someday. Until then, just do as you've been asked, also known as "politely commanded"!

(Note: We joke around and talk like this, so please don't take it too seriously. She certainly doesn't.)

Though she was a little snarky (which I love about her), Anna made an excellent point that you must grapple with if you want to be happy: At any given moment, being selfish seems like the right move. Then again, from the short-term perspective, so does doing drugs and ditching work.

> **GET THIS!**
>
> Self-absorption feels like the right move, but it's a trick because it only works in the short term and results in long-term disaster.

That means the mind might just be *foolish enough to trade long-term traits for short-term states.* Accordingly, my daughter threw a mini tantrum because her mind had been conditioned to (a) focus so intently on herself because her previous experiences around losing sleep had produced emotions that she deemed nearly unbearable, and (b) assume she could continue reaping the benefits of others' unselfishness while being unwilling to offer the same in return.

If it seems like I'm bagging on Anna, I'm not. We're all the same in these ways.

A while later, we had the following interaction.

Me: I know you have a lot of drama in your life, given the developmental stage all of you are in—running an experiment to see if caring an awful lot more about yourselves than others will work as a strategy for happiness. I want you to look at every nasty little drama in your social circle and tell me if the root cause isn't someone caring too much about themselves.

Anna: I know, Dad. It's just a hard transition to make, and being selfish really does feel like the right move a lot of the time, even though I know it isn't. I'll get there someday, but it isn't today.

Ah, the joys of parenting teenagers!

Anna is wicked smart and gets the bigger picture. But as she pointed out, the transition from externally sourced to internally sourced happiness and peace of mind is challenging. I am here to tell you that making this shift will also be the most rewarding and beneficial thing you'll ever do. I promise.

Self-absorption makes conflict and competition inevitable. Notice that the definitions of peace and happiness are subjective: Each individual maintains widely varying views around the circumstances that will lead to pleasure and those that will lead to pain. Individualism and self-absorption inherently lead to competition with other egos trying to achieve the circumstances that will deliver their particular flavor of happiness. This power struggle is why we're often in conflict with each other. We are demanding different things from the same situation!

One person may feel comfortable only when their home is

spotlessly clean. Another person may feel uncomfortable that such a home doesn't even feel lived in. Who's right? Neither. Consequently, when these two people fight about it, "they" are not actually fighting. It's their neurotic demands that are in conflict, based on the fact that the internal condition of comfort is accessible only by proxy of the external conditions. This approach is also why so many friendships and intimate relationships fail: People use each other as pieces of the peace-and-happiness puzzle they are constantly trying to assemble. When another person fails to fulfill the roles they've been hired to perform, they are seen as obstacles that need to be replaced.

FLAWED STRATEGY #3: EMOTIONAL SUPPRESSION AND AVOIDANCE

Since your goals and associated strategies fail to deliver the stable, lasting peace and happiness you desire, you experience dissatisfaction and discontent, so you develop additional strategies to suppress and avoid these states. Not surprisingly, there are inherent problems with this strategy too.

Being a human is intense. We've all heard stories of the mother who summoned the strength to lift a car off her trapped child, a phenomenon psychologists refer to as *hysterical strength*. It's an amazing feature of the human emotional system: When emotions run high enough, the mind and body can produce enough energy to lift a car.

You're dealing with a minor version of this in everyday life. Being an authentic human being in this world is an intense mental and emotional experience, and nothing can change that. Interestingly, you don't actually fear situations; you fear how you're going to feel when they occur. Thus the only viable solution is to learn how to deal with situations by working skillfully with the intensity of your mental and emotional systems.

This ruse is the fundamental issue with toxic masculinity: Emotions are powerful to the point of overwhelm and even panic and trauma, yet people are pretending they're not. Unfortunately, this is also a flawed strategy, because when emotions are disregarded or shoved down instead of being recognized and dealt with appropriately, they have a funny way of leaking out—often with detrimental effect. This ridiculous charade leads to disconnection from the self, disconnection from others, and with some people, an awful lot of alcohol consumption.

> **GET THIS!**
> Being a human is an intense emotional experience, and that can't be changed. The only viable strategy is to master the art of emoting.

Mindlessness is an unmitigated disaster. As your grand plans and misguided efforts continue to be thwarted by such inevitabilities as impermanence and unpredictability, your mind becomes increasingly bogged down by discursive thoughts, fatigue, and frustration. The deleterious effects these have on you, others, and the world have become exacerbated. Incessant and evermore powerful distractions become the only "solution." Social media, television, gambling, gossip, consumption, porn, exercise, work, drugs, and alcohol—distract, distract, distract.

And the most aggressively employed distraction of them all? Incessant rumination, because as long as you're thinking, you aren't fully feeling the extent of your unhappiness or lack of peace.

This avoidance of feeling via incessant thinking is why a majority of beginning meditators all report that, within months, they spontaneously start crying and don't know why. Well, here's why: The mind has failed to achieve stable peace and happiness, and maybe for the first time ever, this sad reality is both undeniable and unavoidable.

Unfortunately, if left unchecked, the result will be the leading of a mindless, unexamined, unconscious, highly defended, inauthentic, addicted, and foolishly unintentional life—the gross, bloody end of ill-defined goals and poorly thought-out strategies. Other than that, Mrs. Lincoln, how was the play?

REDEFINING YOUR GOALS

After over 20 years of study, contemplation, and meditation, I've concluded that happiness and peace of mind are complicated and loaded concepts that lack specificity and mean something different to everyone. Worse yet, the way we have defined them has led to the deployment of inherently flawed strategies that have resulted in unsolvable problems. Instead, I now prefer the following definitions.

- **Joy:** A *state* or *trait* of mind resulting from *a positive relationship* to what's happening (pleasure and pain), based heavily on a particular perspective and grounded in *ataraxis* (a state of serenity, tranquility, contentedness, peace, and ease). It's the opposite of suffering. You've probably never heard of the word *ataraxis* before, which is a shame because it's all you ever wanted (even though you didn't know you wanted it). What a profound irony that a word encapsulating everything everyone wants is so obscure as to be virtually unknown!

- **Suffering:** A *state* or *trait* of mind resulting from a *negative relationship* to what's happening (pleasure and pain), based heavily on a particular perspective and grounded in *affliction* (a state of turmoil, agitation, discontent, anxiety, and stress). It's the opposite of joy.

The goal then is obviously to generate more joy, especially ataraxis, and less suffering. Throughout the book, I'll use all three goals—joy, ataraxis, and the avoidance of suffering—somewhat interchangeably. These definitions are superior because they are internally focused, which means they are completely within your control. In short, you now have a fighting chance of succeeding. You will be trying to directly generate internal states of mind based on internal perspectives and internal relationships to those perspectives. The definitions also point to goals that can be experienced beyond mere temporary states, given that joy and ataraxis can be stabilized into traits *regardless of circumstances*.

Furthermore, just as the original goal definitions led to an obvious strategy, so do these: *Manage your perspectives and relationships to those perspectives*. That's the fundamental issue with the existing goals and strategies: Circumstance management inevitably results in irreparably broken relationships to others, yourself, your mind and emotions, and your life in general.

Now let me be clear. I'm not suggesting that you shouldn't improve your circumstances if you can. Of course you should. I'm suggesting you stop making the mistake of hyper-focusing on generating external states while neglecting the cultivation of stable internal traits. That's the purpose of this book: to convince you that you need to start working *internally*. And I'll show you how to do that by working with your mind and heart directly.

CHANGING YOUR RELATIONSHIPS

It should be clear by now that you don't want temporary states; you want stable traits. Chasing pleasurable circumstances and avoiding painful ones can create positive states but also traps your mind in the negative traits of constant craving and anxiety. The new definitions I just discussed imply that the successful cultivation of positive traits will be determined by *relationships* to things, not by the things themselves.

Pleasure and pain cause the mental and emotional anguish we refer to as "suffering" when you *relate* to them in a particular way—through egoic attachment. But what's that? Attachment describes how an individual relates to something and, consequently, is a manifestation of self-absorption. When you're highly attached to something, it is not a stretch to say that your definition of "self" partially depends upon that thing.

For example, if someone is highly attached to their children, they partially define themselves as a parent and likely even view their children as a reflection of themselves. If someone is highly attached to work outcomes, they partially define themselves as a worker (one who accomplishes outcomes) and value themselves according to the measurable outcomes of their projects. Most people also define themselves in terms of what they like and dislike, directly resulting from their attachment to pleasures.

Attachment is a relationship that turns preferences into demands, which, similar to all forms of addiction, is one of the primary ways it causes so many problems. Before you ask, the answer is yes, I just suggested that we're all attachment-based addicts. What is an addict other than someone who cannot stop chasing after something, even when such pursuit leads to negative and even devastating consequences like anxiety, depression, and conflict? This is why I often refer to Westerners as "comfort addicts" because we demand that everything be just so, and this is the basis of an awful lot of our issues.[10]

In this way, you can view joy and suffering as responses to a specific type of relationship. Accordingly, you can view ataraxis as the result of a radically transformed relationship to both pleasure and pain. This relationship is rooted in *nonattachment*—a fundamental "okayness" with whatever happens to be present in any given moment, in contrast to attachment that results in craving and aversion. Nonattachment can *feel* like not caring, but that isn't the case, because if you didn't care, you wouldn't work hard to achieve a particular outcome. We are carefully separating what needs to be done from how you feel doing it, which can be accomplished because acceptance and tolerance (emotional responses based in nonattachment) are not the same as complacence (a behavioral response). A solution is starting to come into view.

RECOGNIZING THAT PLEASURE ≠ HAPPINESS, BUT IT'S STILL WONDERFUL

Many people react with extreme aversion to what I have been saying about pleasure, voicing disputes along the lines of "You mean I'm not supposed to enjoy pleasurable things? And we're all supposed to give up everything and be some kind of monk or nun? Screw that!" Right, my "practical solution" to all our problems requires everyone to give up pleasure and become a wandering mendicant. No, obviously that's not what I mean.

The thing is *never* the problem; your relationship to the thing is *always* the problem. In an attempt to avoid cognitive distortions, I try not to use superlatives like "never" and "always," but in this case, they're appropriate. Pleasure isn't a problem unless incessant craving drives your relationship with it, leading to suffering. The fact that the human body and mind are capable of experiencing pleasure is not a bad thing in and of itself. In fact, it's a beautiful thing. Our problem is that we become so wholly reliant on pleasure due to attachment.

RECOGNIZING THAT PAIN ≠ SUFFERING

Just as there's nothing wrong with pleasure, other than your attachment-based relationship to it that creates the suffering of craving, there's nothing wrong with pain, other than your attachment-based relationship to its absence that creates the suffering of aversion. Pain becomes a problem when it is experienced along with states of meaninglessness, hopelessness, helplessness, aloneness, and/or overwhelm, which results in suffering and even trauma. Absent these states, pain can result in joy; just ask any high-performing athlete. Bible verse James 1:2–4 states, "Consider it pure joy, my brothers and sisters, whenever you face trials of many kinds, because you know that the testing of your faith produces *perseverance*."

Note that the ability to persevere through hardship is a relationship-based *trait* of mind, not a *state*, so they had it right. Your relationship to pain can currently be described as one of hatred, not only because it doesn't feel good, but because it implies that your strategy has failed yet again. To the attached pleasure-seeker, pain and discomfort are enemies that must be avoided at all costs. However, for all the reasons already mentioned, pain cannot be avoided in every circumstance, nor can it be if you aim to achieve stable joy/ataraxis and avoid suffering.

As newly defined, suffering arises from your relationship to pain and represents your belief-based demand that reality be different than it is. Thus the internal cause of suffering is usually easy to identify, because all you have to do is identify the demand-based belief behind it, which will be associated with a "should" or "supposed to" or "ought to." Ask yourself why "should" circumstances be the way you say. They "should" be your way so you don't have to deal with the pain and suffering you experience when they're not.

For example, a conversation might be painful, but the hours you spend replaying it for no reason other than to justify your anger is suffering. Consequently, people come to believe that conversations *should* not be painful. I've had to teach nearly every client that "peace of mind" is *not* the absence of negative emotions but rather a relationship of total acceptance and nonresistance to whatever state arises.

Avoiding pain and discomfort also prevents you from accomplishing much of what you want in life. Healthy eating, exercising, studying for school, avoiding excessive drug and alcohol use, prying yourself away from your phone at night, and working hard on tedious tasks to support a successful career all require the acceptance of daily pain and discomfort that the comfort addict seeks to avoid. This is how we arrived at idiotic concepts like work/life balance, as if work is somehow not your life. I'm technically "working" right now, and it sure feels like it's part of my life. In short, you simply cannot achieve wellness with a strategy based on pain and discomfort avoidance. It's impossible and sets up a war you can't win.

ACTUALLY DO THIS

I've read many books that included practices throughout each chapter, and—full disclosure—I glanced at most of them but never really engaged. What a foolish mistake. So please take a minute and actually do these things. Seriously. As one of my therapy mentors said frequently, "If nothing changes, nothing changes!" You need to practice to allow yourself to change.

1. Check in with yourself. What is your current *state* of mind? What is your current *state* of heart—that is, what emotion(s) is (are) most dominant for you? (*Pause.*)

2. Next, investigate the current *trait* being actively cultivated by inspecting how your mind is *relating* to this moment. You have two choices:

    A. The mind is cultivating *trait craving*—a thought-based judgment of the present moment via comparison to all other possible moments. This mode of thinking could include possibly looking forward to it changing, thus projecting the mind into the future and away from the present.

> B. The mind is cultivating *trait equanimity* by resting in "the now," absent judgmental comparison, fully accepting whatever *states* happen to be present, and thus experiencing freedom from craving and aversion. To get here, shift into radical acceptance, as I taught you in Chapter 0, and deeply engage the present moment without resistance. The present moment is never bothering you. You're bothering *it*, so just stop and allow your mind to *be*. Now SNAP!
>
> *Extra Credit If You Are an Overachiever:* Can you readily switch back and forth between the trait cultivation modes of craving and equanimity?

TAKING EMOTIONAL RESPONSIBILITY

All emotions are more representative of your relationship to what is happening than what's actually happening. This can be observed directly in people's widely varying reactions to the same perceived circumstances. For example, my boss once returned from a customer meeting and informed the team that he had signed us up for an impossible project. Yes, impossible, given that success would've required bending the laws of physics on an aggressive schedule. That night, I complained to my wife about how stressful the next year would be. But when I arrived at the office the following day, I found a colleague at his desk unusually early because he couldn't sleep with all his excitement over this new challenge. Where he saw an exciting opportunity, I saw a stressful and inevitable failure, and I experienced severe anxiety over what it would mean for me personally and professionally.

So here's the money question: How did it make sense to claim that the events *caused* my stressful reaction if they simultaneously *caused* a nearly opposite response for someone else? Were the meeting and project exciting and invigorating, or were they stressful? Something wasn't making sense, because scientifically, if the same factor produces opposite outcomes, it can't be a *cause* of either! My stress and anxiety arose directly from my troubled internal relationships with the project and myself, just as my colleague's joy arose directly from his positive internal relationships with the same set of circumstances.

When describing an emotional situation, people often blame their feelings on external causes with phrases using the verb *make* as in "This printer is making me mad today!" It would be alright if I never heard this ridiculously disempowering framing again.

In recent years, I've heard people using the word *triggered*, which I prefer because it indicates that the person's mind—the thing that got triggered—is at least somehow involved. External circumstances contribute to the arising of emotions, but they do not cause them.

> **GET THIS!**
>
> Nothing and no one can make you feel any particular way, because feelings arise as a direct result of your internal relationship to circumstances and not the circumstances themselves.

Emotional responsibility is hard to accept for two primary reasons. First, it can be painfully difficult to see that, throughout your life, your mind has been effectively causing its own suffering. In other words, you have been much less the victim of circumstances and much more the perpetrator, and that's an awfully jagged pill to choke down. Second, you want to have something or someone to blame; otherwise, the work is for you to do.

You should take responsibility, because if circumstances caused your emotional reactions, you'd be doomed for all the reasons outlined in this chapter—lack of adequate control, impermanence, interdependence, and insatiability. I know how hard emotional responsibility is to see, let alone accept. Still, it's crucial that you do so, because you won't make progress until this basic fact of life is firmly embedded in your mind and begins to transform how you interact with yourself and your world.

> **GET THIS!**
> As painful as it is, being wholly responsible for your emotional states—blaming nothing and no one else—is the only way to fly; otherwise, you'll always be a victim.

When confused people experience difficulty, they look to the situation and others for what's wrong. When wise people working toward authentic wellness interact with difficulty, they look internally at both their *perceptions* and their *relationship* to those perceptions, and spend the time and effort to alter both.

CHAPTER HIGHLIGHTS

To sum things up, you have failed to achieve mental, emotional, and physical wellbeing in your life because you adopted ill-defined goals that were impossible to achieve, which led to failed strategies that turned you into some version of an anxiety-ridden comfort addict. None of this is a big deal because there are perfectly viable solutions.

With sound goals and a closely associated high-level strategy now defined, I'm sure you want to get right to the specific strategies and tactics that will work. Unfortunately, you aren't quite ready for that. Any engineer will tell you that until you understand and resolve a problem's root cause, you're only putting Band-Aids on the symptoms. You aren't going to do that. You're ripping the Band-Aids off, not putting more on.

Next you're going to learn the root cause of why you developed flawed goals and futile strategies, to ensure you don't make the same mistakes again. So please bear with me for one more chapter, and then I'll get to the happier stuff.

Key Insights

- Reliance on circumstances may lead to temporary positive *states* of mind, but it will also directly cause the *traits* of anxiety and incessant craving and aversion. In this way, you should view any moments of happiness and peace of mind as fleeting "breaks" from the underlying trait anxiety, craving, and aversion you feel, which drives your demand for control and prevents you from fully relaxing into yourself and your life.

- You have incorrectly concluded that pleasure and pain are equivalent to happiness and suffering, respectively.

- Pleasure and pain are circumstantial, but circumstances are too unstable due to impermanence, unpredictability, and a lack of adequate control over them, which inevitably leads to the trait of anxiety—an afflicted relationship with reality.

- Chasing after particular states and running away from others—also known as "circumstance management"—doesn't work and causes many other problems for which you developed additional mitigation strategies. Furthermore, those strategies cause yet additional problems like emotional irresponsibility, aggressive competition and conflict, an inability to fully experience the emotional intensity of human life, and mindlessness, all of which combine to create still more problems!

- Avoiding pain and discomfort causes you to lack self-discipline, thus making the achievement of mental, emotional, and physical wellbeing an arduous venture that fails repeatedly.

- You actually want positive *traits*, which manifest in the way you relate to internal and external, positive and negative states. You chase after *states* because you have failed to cultivate the traits of mind you would enjoy.

- You now have a soundly defined goal of achieving joy, which automatically implies avoiding their opposite—suffering. You have also defined a sound high-level strategy for their achievement: managing internal perspectives and relationships to those perspectives, both of which can come under volitional control.

- The arising of joy/ataraxis and the avoidance of suffering will require you to take complete emotional responsibility for yourself, which is challenging.

Assessing Flawed Goals and Ineffective Strategies

You now know where you want to head—in the direction of ever-increasing, stable joy and ataraxis. In Chapter 2, you'll learn about how your mind works and discover the Great Self. With these new understandings of how the mind functions, you will start to develop strategies for reaching your goal.

CHAPTER 2

DISCOVERING YOUR GREAT SELF

> Recognizing truth requires selflessness. You have to leave yourself out of it so you can find out the way things are in themselves, not the way they look to you or how you feel about them or how you would like them to be.
>
> — HARRY FRANKFURT

At this point in your journey, you've explored a working theory of what's wrong: You habitually relate to life's experiences in a way that inevitably generates constantly varying mental states of stress, anxiety, craving, fear, and mindless rumination. Over time, these fleeting states increasingly solidify into ingrained traits, shaping how you perceive and interact with yourself and the world. To avoid building your immaculate new home on the same unstable foundation, you need to understand why otherwise sane people would engage in such self-defeating behaviors. To move forward with confidence that you can achieve your goal of cultivating joy and ataraxis by prioritizing enduring traits over fleeting emotional states, you must investigate the basis of the broken traits—the source of the flawed perceptions of and relationships to others, yourself, your life, and even reality itself. By exposing the root cause of your failed attempts to find ataraxis, the solution will become evident.

To arrive at the root cause and its solution, this chapter starts by explaining how a human being constructs a reality and defines themselves within it. Though the explanation is a bit technical, I know you can understand it, so please trust yourself intellectually and *take your time with the material.* I hope you'll enjoy learning about yourself and how your mind constructs and experiences reality, not only because it's fascinating, but also because it's the most consequential and transformational lesson you'll ever learn. If that sounds like a bold claim, I hope you'll see how this is possible by the end of this chapter.

Achieving joy and ataraxis is surprisingly straightforward with the right approach—and impossible without it. But you're in luck, because I'm going to give you the manual, and if you take the time to read it with an open mind, then in less than an hour, you will understand more about your own peace, happiness, and reality than probably anyone you know. You'll be like a Jedi knight from *Star Wars* with all your new mind tricks, and who wouldn't want that?

COMPONENTS OF THE HUMAN MENTAL AND SENSORY SYSTEM

To discuss any system's operation, we typically start by modeling it, and that's what we're going to build for the human mental and sensory system. To create this model of reality and the sense of an "I" operating within it, we must begin with the cornerstone of experience itself, consciousness, which is defined for our purposes as a process that generates a unique flavor of experience from a particular physical phenomenon. This may differ somewhat from more classical definitions of this term.

In his seminal 1974 essay "What Is It Like to Be a Bat?,"[11] philosopher Thomas Nagel defined consciousness as "it's like something." It's like something to see red and like something else to see blue, but because of consciousness, it's always like *something*. In other words, *an experience is happening*, and it must be *like something* to be having it. Dr. Nagel asserted that despite it being difficult for humans to imagine what it's like to have the faculty of sonar-based echolocation, it must be like something to have it—a type of experience.

If an object isn't conscious, it isn't like anything to be it, which implies that the object you refer to as "me" is much more than just a bunch of chemistry and physics. For example, chemistry and physics can be used to describe the process of seeing. Photons pass through a lens and some weird jelly before hitting the retina, which triggers biochemical reactions that convert light into electricity (a process called phototransduction). This electricity then travels to the brain's visual cortex, causing hundreds of millions of neurons to vibrate electrically based on the color of the light. While that's interesting, it does nothing to explain why this cascade of physical phenomena gives rise to the experience of seeing—why it's like something, or anything for that matter, for neurons to fire in a particular way. I can also describe a car engine's operation using chemistry and physics. Gas, air, and electricity combine in the process of combustion,

> **GET THIS!**
>
> Consciousness means "It's like something."

the force of which is used to move a piston. Does that mean the engine is having an experience? Probably not!

A scientist scanning my brain could say, "Joe is currently seeing the color he's been taught to call blue," but they cannot measure the actual image presented to my local awareness. The experience is uniquely mine alone and cannot be measured directly, because it isn't a material thing but a hallucination of sorts. In other words, the atoms in a blue object are not blue; blue is merely a label for the experience produced when 450-nanometer light excites human visual consciousness. And each individual maintains their own version of it. In other words, an electromagnetic wave of light does not have the quality of color, because color is something made by human consciousness in response to a particular kind of excitation. That is why, in the first sentence of this paragraph, I said, "Joe is currently seeing the color *he's been taught to call* blue."

Blue is not a universal truth, property, or characteristic of the electromagnetic wave; it's a description of a human experience.

Most people are aware of the five most common types of "it's like something" that produce the myriad varieties of human conscious experience.

- Auditory (sound)
- Visual (sight)
- Olfactory (smell)
- Gustatory (taste)
- Tactile (touch)

To deepen your understanding of consciousness, consider other types of sensory consciousness that exist, such as the echolocation consciousness enjoyed by dolphins and bats. We didn't get that one, but dolphins and bats don't enjoy our visual system: Humans are capable of perceiving over a million unique colors! Animals also aren't (likely) experiencing the same depth and complexity of consciousness that humans can in particular ways. A couple of those ways will be essential to understand, so let's cover two of them now: the sixth and seventh consciousnesses.

UNDERSTANDING THE SIXTH CONSCIOUSNESS: MENTAL

We distinguish mental activity as a separate type of consciousness because you can view thoughts as mental sensations produced by the brain, just as you perceive tastes as gustatory sensations produced by the tongue.

The sixth consciousness operates on constructs—abstract ideas about things and not the actual things themselves—to support the construction of reality. A typical example that illustrates how constructs are merely relative representations and not an accurate picture of reality is that of a seed, sprout, sapling, and tree. If you look up these terms, you will find no precise, uniform definition for exactly when one of these stages ends and the next begins. I ran this experiment and looked up *sapling* and *mature tree* and found one definition stating that a sapling becomes a mature tree when its trunk reaches 2.75 inches in diameter. Another definition states that a sapling becomes a mature tree only when it produces flowers.

Can you see how we arbitrarily assign boundaries, impose them upon the natural world, and then take them to be factual? From nature's perspective, none of these things exist. There is just a continuum of change. The sapling only exists in a relative way—

relative to a defined seedling on one side and a defined mature tree on the other. Thus "sapling" is simply an idea—a construct we use to create and organize our story of reality.

To make sense of the world, our minds make distinctions and categorize phenomena based on our perceptions. Furthermore, our perceptions—take vision, for example—depend upon things like distance from the perceived object, magnification level, and visible light spectrum. Our descriptions are more about *how* we're looking than *what* we're looking at. The key point is that your mind constructs your current experience of the world by imputing ideas onto reality. It's crucial to remember that mental constructs and the concepts about them that follow point at things but are *not* the things themselves, because the "things" are a direct conscious experience, not an imaginary idea about them. As such, you are removed from reality *as it is* by these thought-based, conceptual overlays.

At this point, some cognitive dissonance might arise as you try to figure out what the heck any of this has to do with joy, ataraxis, or suffering. Well, let's look at an example from a therapy session I was doing with a client who had anger issues.

> *Joe:* You seem awfully angry about the game's outcome on Sunday.
>
> *Client (highly animated):* You wouldn't believe the mistakes the Broncos made—it was total amateur hour out there! And as for the jagoff refs—don't even get me started. They were playing for the Chiefs! And it sucks, because we're probably not going to the playoffs now.

Joe: Strange question, but does football exist in nature?

Client (pondering): No, obviously not. We drew a bunch of lines on the grass and made up some rules.

Joe: Why did we do that?

Client: I don't know—I guess we were bored. (*Pause.*) Oh my gosh—I see it. I'm literally pissed off over the thing we made up because we were bored, and now I'm suffering over it.

Joe: Right, you're suffering fundamentally because you— (*Client cuts me off.*)

Client: —forgot that it was all made-up in the first place! My gosh, that helps. But I feel so foolish and immature now!

Joe: Well, there's no need for that, nor is it helpful. Humans have never suffered for any reason other than believing in made-up stories that ultimately aren't true.

Client: Shit, that's deep. I'm gonna have to think about that one!

Joe: I've been thinking about it for the last twenty years!

You suffer daily over made-up stories because your mind forgets that you made them up in the first place. The fact that others provide you with scripts throughout your life, which form the basis of these stories, changes nothing. In other words, constructs are often useful fictions, but they become harmful when you forget that they are nothing more than mere ideas. The mind takes raw sensory data it receives from phenomena, busily fabricates meaningful stories about them, and then suffers over the constructed reality it creates as if it wasn't the source of it all. How could suffering be explained any other way, given that one mind suffers in a particular situation while another thrives in the same circumstance? It can only be because minds construct different stories and derive different meanings from them. When you directly experience this truth, your mind will feel as if someone has pulled it back from the screen of a terrifying movie.

> **GET THIS!**
> Based on how it is observing, your mind applies constructs to reality and then forms stories with those constructs... but then forgets that it's the one making the story.

UNDERSTANDING THE SEVENTH CONSCIOUSNESS: EGO FUNCTION IDENTIFICATION

It isn't hard to accept that we're each part of a larger whole, inextricably interconnected and interdependent with all that exists. You are what you eat, drink, and breathe, and molecules produced from within your body are inside every tree you've ever seen. There are trillions of organisms—more of them than all the other cells in your body—sustaining themselves by living inside your body. People, animals, plants, and many other organisms affect you physically, psychologically, and emotionally, just as you similarly affect them.

Perhaps you have had the intuitive experience that your mind appears part of a more complex and magnificent whole—sometimes referred to as "universal consciousness"—in which case, interconnectedness may not be so challenging to grasp. Even without this experience, some open-minded and earnest investigation will likely yield at least an inclination into the deep interconnectedness and interdependence of our existence. And if you're still not sold, imagine what it would be like to exist without relying on other people, animals, or the environment. Next time you eat, think about how many animals (like bees) and people (like accountants and truck drivers) were required to put that food on your plate. It's overwhelming when you see it. In doing this, you will understand that total physical, mental, and emotional separation from the world is impossible and, therefore, ultimately illusory.

That said, just as you aren't entirely separate, you're also not wholly unified or "all one" either. For example, your eating obviously doesn't nourish my body. Additionally, the caution you showed by putting your seat belt on won't protect me in the event of an accident. Thus each of us must be concerned for our own wellbeing and survival. Therefore, the brain must contain a function that asserts *I'm a mind within a body, small and separate in important ways and responsible for meeting my needs by manipulating the world around me to ensure my safety and survival.*

We refer to this as the *ego function*. And without it, we all would've been dead long ago.

The last function of mind you need to be concerned with is the process of identification. This is how you come to define and know your "self"—the collection of phenomena you refer to as either "me" or "mine." The process is highly contextual and socially constructed, because your mind learns what to identify with from others who have also been conditioned by various factors.

For example, you likely strongly identify with your physical body, beliefs, and thoughts, as well as your closely associated personalities, temperamental traits, emotions, desires, aversions, and even the roles you play, such as "father" or "nurse." Your mind primarily associates itself with those things because that's how the ego function defines itself. The ego function takes the *perspective* that it *is* the small, separate thing and relates to the world accordingly. Once the mind identifies with the ego function (as in, I am that), the small self is now "born" and the being relates to itself, others, and the world in general from the ego function's afflicted perspective, which is a disaster. (If these ideas remain a bit murky for you, please don't fret; they'll clear up as we proceed.)

> **GET THIS!**
>
> The afflicted (seventh) consciousness arises as a result of ego function identification. This is how the small self is "born."

We identify the ego function as a type of consciousness because experiencing reality from its perspective is certainly like something. It's so deeply ingrained that it mediates, flavors, or alters all experiences through thoughts, stories, and emotions.

I'm guessing you have experienced that person who immediately turns every conversation to themselves. This behavior is due to the ego function's unchecked operation. Their mind constantly interprets all experiences solely from the perspective of the self, as in "How does this relate to *me*? What do *I* think, how do *I* feel, and what do *I* need to do about this?" It's not that they don't care about you; their minds have been hijacked by ego function identification, causing them to process everything through a self-absorbed lens. So there's no need to take it personally.

COMPARING AWARENESS AND CONSCIOUSNESS

We need to make one last subtle distinction before completing our model. Conscious experiences must be known by something, and that's where awareness enters the picture. People often use the terms *awareness* and *consciousness* interchangeably because it's almost impossible to imagine one without the other. Let's explore awareness and how it differs from consciousness, keeping in mind that for our purposes, awareness is defined as the knowing or cognizant aspect of mind.

Think of your awareness as the screen reflecting the conscious, mind-made movie of your life. The reason we need to separate consciousness and awareness is hugely significant: Awareness is not only aware of conscious experiences but is also aware *of itself*. Clients sometimes get hung up on this idea of awareness being aware of itself because it sounds complicated at first. Let's clear that up.

You get awareness for free. You can't stop your mind from being aware for even a second. For example, your mind is clearly still aware of sound when you're asleep; otherwise, I wouldn't be able to wake you up by shouting at you. Awareness is always present, but *what* it is aware of changes constantly.

Now let's try to help you click into awareness of awareness. First, simply become aware of the fact that you are reading a book. Next, try and click one more channel over: Can you be aware that you are aware that you are reading a book? It helped me to replace the word *aware* with the word *know*, so let's try that now. You know you are reading a book. Do you know that you *know* you are reading a book? Take a second or two to investigate. The risk is in making it too complicated, so just say to yourself "Yes, of course, I know I'm reading a book. And of course I know that I *know* that." That's awareness of awareness, or knowing of knowingness.

MODELING THE SMALL SELF

We now have everything we need to build our model of the human mental and sensory systems, as shown in Figure 2.1. The model is called the Small-Self Perspective because the mind has identified with the ego function that sees itself as small, fragile, inadequate, alone, and insecure, which leads to beings seeing themselves in these same afflicted ways. The word *small* also describes how the being's mind feels—tight, confined, and claustrophobic. Ideologically captured by the sixth and seventh consciousnesses, this is the constrained space in which most people currently exist.

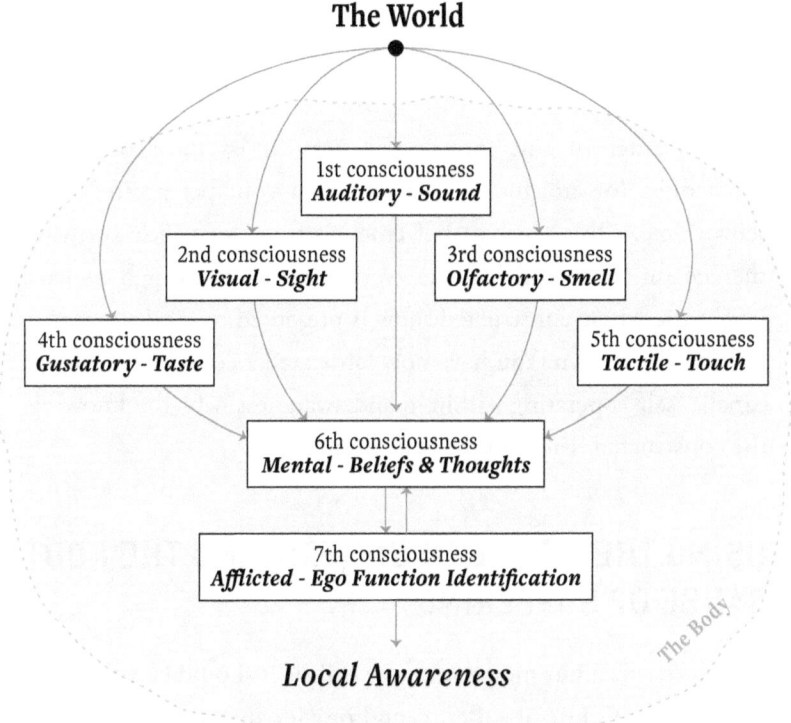

Figure 2.1 *Model of Human Mental and Sensory Systems— Small-Self Perspective*

Notice that all the arrows in the model flow in one direction, except for the second arrow from the bottom, showing how the afflicted (seventh) consciousness profoundly shapes the thoughts and beliefs of the mental (sixth) consciousness.

The world enters the body (the shaded area) and mind through the five sense consciousnesses. This is how you perceive all external stimuli. However, the tactile (fifth) consciousness also perceives internally generated tactile sensations—the critical foundation of all emotional experiences—just as the auditory (first) consciousness also processes internally generated sounds. The brain funnels all sensory inputs (external and internal) to the mental (sixth) consciousness, where the raw data is formed into constructs, shaping the narrative you call "reality."

At the center of this meaningful story is its most persistent protagonist (or antagonist, depending on your perspective), the self or "me." This sense of self emerges from identification with the ego function, which filters every experience through its lens. Lastly, the whole constructed show is presented to local awareness so it can be known. You have now fabricated a conscious reality, a (small) "self" operating within it, and awareness, which is knowing the constructed reality in the background.

USING THE MODEL TO UNDERSTAND THE ROOT CAUSE OF SUFFERING

As advertised, if our model is of any utility, it should be able to explain the root cause of suffering and provide direction on possible solutions. Let's quickly review the revised definition of suffering: a state or *trait* of mind resulting from a negative *relationship* to what's happening (pleasure and pain), based heavily on a *particular perspective* and grounded in affliction.

Thus suffering is caused by *relationships* to *perspectives*, so we need to investigate how the mind forms perspectives and develops relationships to them when organized according to the current model, as shown in Figure 2.1. Remember that the mind is identified with the ego function, as modeled by the afflicted (seventh) consciousness, so we are particularly concerned about that function's perspectives and relationships.

Here are a few of the more important ones.

- I'm either the body itself, as in "I am dying," or its owner, as in "My knee hurts."

- I'm either the thinking mind, as in "I am very scatterbrained today," or its owner, as in "My thoughts are racing."

- I'm either the emotions, as in "I am sad," or their owner, as in "My anger is raging."

- I'm a victim of a reality that's happening *to me*, so I experience trait anxiety without respite.

- I come to know myself, others, and the world exclusively through my thoughts and beliefs—the constructed stories woven by the mental (sixth) consciousness.

Notice the first and most common word in every single perspective is "I" because the ego function experiences everything *by referring all conscious phenomena back to itself.* This way of relating to phenomena is the small-minded self, which is the root cause of all suffering.

HOW SELF-ABSORPTION IMPACTS DAILY LIFE

If ego function identification is the root problem, self-absorption is the worst symptom due to its impact on every aspect of life. Remember that the ego function is how our brains evolved to survive—by defining the "self" as a mind somehow contained inside a body, separate from the environment. From this fundamental idea of separation comes the belief that protecting against and manipulating others and the world around us is necessary.

From this perspective, we are constantly in some degree of a fight-or-flight response.

The origin of the ego function's self-absorption dates all the way back to the origins of life itself. Natural selection is an inherently self-absorbed approach to survival, essentially dictating that each being must compete for the prize of having their genetic code continue the species. Through that competition, physical and mental traits are in a continual state of optimization, yielding organisms that are ever-better at doing one thing: surviving long enough to pass their genes on successfully.

Notice this clearly stated objective does not include being joyful (as long as you aren't so miserable that others don't want to reproduce with you). The ego function's job is to preserve and protect, and to do that, it employs the mental (sixth) consciousness to compute solutions to avoid or solve problems. And it always finds problems. The ego believes it is under constant threat whether actual (physical) or existential (intangible), which is one reason it's so challenging to stop yourself from thinking.

Evolution doesn't care the slightest bit if you experience joy and avoid suffering; it only cares that you survive. If you worry nearly incessantly about yourself and those in your tribe, thus leading to improved chances of survival, all the better. As for those in the distant past who heard lions growling in the forest and didn't worry about it…well, let's just say they didn't survive to become our ancestors. This means you're deeply programmed to be anxious through your evolutionarily driven genetic code. Moreover, evolution seems to prioritize short-term survival over long-term wellbeing. After all, there's no point in long-term plans if you don't survive today. This prioritization presents a real problem, because trait wellbeing requires seeing the big picture and prioritizing the long term over the short term. Such prioritization inevitably entails discomfort, and the ego function wants no part of that.

Here's the thing: If evolution dictates that the survival and propagation of our genes take precedence over others', and emotions reflect our chances of passing on those genes, then it directly follows that *our emotions are also correspondingly more important.* And since we identify with an ego function that experiences emotions as an integral part of itself, we thus *perceive ourselves as more important than others*. Sure, we want others to do well…just not as well as ourselves.

You must bravely look as deeply as possible into yourself to see if this is true. Isn't your happiness and wellbeing just a bit more important to you than almost everyone else's? Even if you consider yourself a relatively selfless person, unless you've subjugated your ego, it's pretty likely that being "unselfish" is your particular flavor of self-absorption. To demonstrate, here's a fun exchange between a certain unnamed someone and my wife Jami that exemplifies how selfishness can masquerade as unselfishness.

> *Unnamed Someone:* What does Joe want for Christmas?
>
> *Jami:* Joe doesn't like stuff. He'd prefer a gift card for an experience, like a dinner or baseball game.
>
> *Unnamed Someone:* But I don't like giving gift certificates. I want to buy him something.
>
> *Jami:* Again, he's repeatedly stated for years now that he doesn't want things and is rather adamant about it.

> *Unnamed Someone: I* just want to enjoy *my* Christmas!

To be fair, not all forms of selfishness are created equal. The flavor of selfishness that seeks approval and self-esteem by doing things for others' sake is often a step in the right direction. At least it's a step up from the self-absorbed beings who only think about themselves. Regardless, no matter the flavor, suffering always represents an "egoic demand that reality be different than it is," which includes the desire to feel better about oneself by doing good things for others.

Remember that no matter what we do, we'll continue to experience pain and discomfort because that's how the mind works. Given that phenomena produce different experiences, the mind will always judge some as better or worse than others. This judgment-based classification happens automatically and cannot be stopped. However, you can stop the real problem: turning both pleasurable and painful experiences into suffering through incessant craving and aversion, along with the ego function's relentless and insatiable need to manipulate circumstances according to its demands accordingly.

To get to the nuclear core of the issue, think of all that follows from the belief that you're a highly loving but neurotic mind contained somewhere inside a tiny meat vehicle. It means that you're small, alone, inadequate, of questionable value—and possibly worst of all—insecure and therefore easily harmed physically, psychologically, and emotionally. These underlying beliefs drive how you relate to others, yourself, and your life.

These troubled relationships with experience—aloneness, fragility/insecurity, powerlessness, and inadequacy—are known as *core vul-*

nerabilities. Anxiety arises when the mind perceives its wellbeing to be dependent on circumstances beyond its control. Stress stems from the mind's belief that its available resources and capabilities are insufficient to meet the demands of a particular situation. Loneliness inevitably arises from the mind's belief in its isolation.

This is why people try to stay busy or are prone to distraction. No amount of external "accomplishment" can change the fact that you feel small and incomplete in your core. This faulty strategy is why it is so hard to get off the hedonic treadmill, constantly chasing pleasure and avoiding pain and fear. These feelings are also why your mind (initially) hates being alone with itself in meditation as an ego trying to function without distractions to help it avoid suffering. That kind of mind is an incredibly afflicted place to be, which is why Buddhists refer to the seventh consciousness as "afflicted."

> **GET THIS!**
> The core vulnerabilities of aloneness, fragility/insecurity, powerlessness, and inadequacy arise as a direct result of ego function identification.

Please ponder that for a few minutes, and then take a 4–7–8 breath, because this is heavy. The good news is that there's a solution coming next!

MODELING THE GREAT SELF

Keeping your eyes on the prize, your primary goal is joy—a state or trait of mind resulting from a positive relationship to what's happening (pleasure and pain), based heavily on a particular perspective and grounded in ataraxis. It is the opposite of suffering.

Once again, the problem surfaces as your perspectives and your relationships to those perspectives. Now that you've arrived at the root cause of the issues you are dealing with, a high-level solution emerges immediately. In defining the term *ego*, Western psychologists combined the ego function and the process of identifying with it. This was a tragic mistake, because this one move—identification with the ego function and all the afflicted, self-referential thought patterns it generates—inevitably results in all the negative consequences mentioned previously. Figure 2.2 introduces the Great Self perspective by rearranging the model of being in a human mind and body.

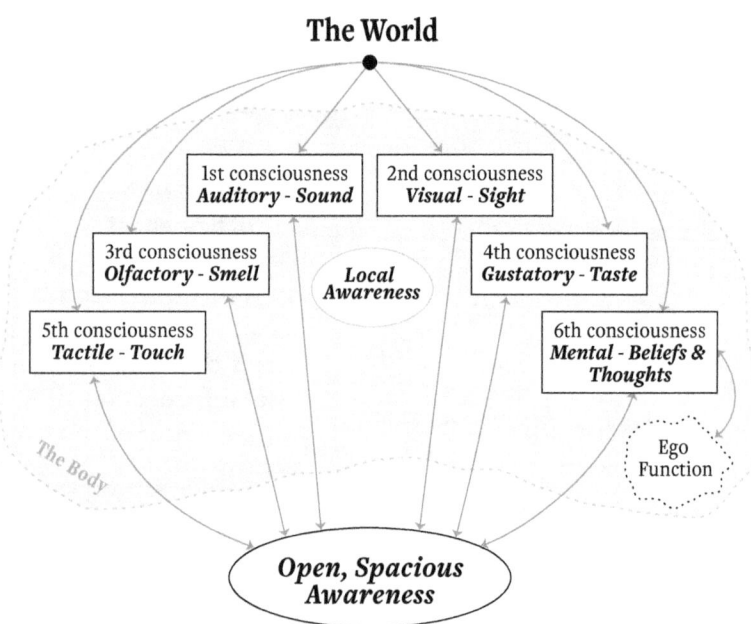

Figure 2.2 *Model of Human Mental and Sensory Systems: Great Self Perspective*

Notice how awareness interacts with conscious phenomena directly without mediation by the mental (sixth) and afflicted (seventh) consciousnesses.

The Great Self arises when the consciousnesses, especially the mental (sixth) consciousness, are managed by awareness instead of the ego function. Awareness is formless, so it needs help operating in the world—assistance that is provided by the physical body and its various consciousnesses. Shifting from small self to Great Self gives you an entirely new perspective on and relationship to reality—one rooted in ataraxis instead of anxiety. Your mind will no longer experience itself as a victim of a reality happening *to it* but rather as a participant in the *co-creation* of reality (along with other minds). The vulnerable child-like ego function, with all its fear-based demands, will now be in its proper place as a helpful promoter of safety and wellbeing through well-managed thoughts and emotions that are no longer overwhelming.

Here are a few key points on the radically different perspectives and relationships to them as produced by the revised model.

- While the world continues entering through the five sensory consciousnesses, experiences no longer invariably pass through the mental (sixth) consciousness and its soap opera. Awareness now *relates* to conscious phenomena in a *direct* and *bidirectional* way (arrows now point in both directions, as shown in Figure 2.2). That means you don't have to live at the mercy of all your afflicted stories by thinking all day, every day, because doing so is nothing short of an unnecessary and avoidable catastrophe, given the effects on one's daily experience of life.

- The ego function (bottom right of Figure 2.2) continues operating but is no longer related to the identification process and, therefore, no longer mediates all experiences. This reorganization dissolves the afflicted (seventh) consciousness, which is huge because it's the source of all suffering. Evolution designed this function to keep you safe; you were never meant to live in it full-time, yet you do, and that's a minor tragedy. Sure, the ego function will continue to judge everything and whine about much of it, but its afflicted relationship to phenomena will no longer dominate the mental landscape.

In other words, the ego's "problems" only become significant when the mind identifies with the ego function, thus making them "your" problems. The mental (sixth) consciousness can still register the ego function's concerns for itself and its body and respond accordingly, but these concerns will no longer be the loudest thing in the room.

Western psychologists have caught wind of this Eastern approach to wellbeing and refer to it as "hypo-egoic self-processes." Their research has concluded that "intentionally trying to control one's behavior sometimes reduces the likelihood of achieving one's goals."[12]

- You can continue to experience awareness in a local way (see the small, mobile bubble in the center of Figure 2.2), but you can also experience it as vast, open, and spacious (see bottom of the figure)—an option previously unavailable. This radical shift in perspective changes how the mind relates to ego-based thoughts and emotions, experiencing them as a less significant part of the overall experience. When awareness is allowed to collapse in on self-absorbed thoughts and emotions, they aren't just the loudest thing in the space—they are the *only* thing. Lacking a more eloquent way to say it, that sucks! It's the only reason you ever feel overwhelmed by an emotional experience and don't sleep as well as you could.

I'll be introducing you to practices that enable you to shift from local awareness to open, spacious awareness (and back again), because you must learn to free yourself from the afflicted experiences of the sixth and seventh consciousnesses.

COMPETING IDENTITIES OF THE SMALL SELF AND GREAT SELF

I've now defined two possible but mutually exclusive (that is, they can't exist simultaneously) identities based on two different objects of identification. If the mind identifies with the ego function, it is small, fragile, and afraid by definition, which is why we refer to that construction as the *small self*. But when the mind identifies with awareness, it is vast and spacious by definition, which is why we refer to that construction as the *Great Self*.

The Great Self and its awareness go by various names depending on the tradition: unchanging self, soul, core being, core self, ground of being, true self, true nature, Buddha-nature, the not-self self, the "I am," and open-hearted awareness, among others. It doesn't matter what label you prefer. I just picked one that wasn't religious and described not only the being but the experience, because it's great to rest as the Great Self!

Let's take a quick break from theory and make all this identity business practical and experiential. The point of it all is actually quite straightforward: Get out of your head (the mind of the small self) and into your life. Constantly thinking, comparing, planning, judging, and worrying as a small self is simply a terrible way to go through life. Incessant rumination represents a wall between your mind and your life; you are living in your stories instead of experiencing your life directly. Reality does not need your conceptual overlay; it doesn't care what you think! This is *the* fundamental mistake and why you don't experience joy and ataraxis frequently throughout your day.

By shifting into your Great Self, you will no longer live in your head but instead experience your life directly, as exemplified in one of my favorite Buddhist parables. Note: In this story, you are looking for *thinking* (sixth consciousness) and *judgment* (seventh consciousness) that would indicate the presence of the small self.

> A young monk noticed an old monk going for a walk at sundown every day and asked to attend. But the old monk refused to allow it, saying, "You aren't ready yet. Go meditate for a year, and then we'll try."
>
> A year passed, and the skeptical old monk allowed the young monk to go on the walk as agreed. They reached the peak of a hill just as the sun touched the horizon, at which point the young monk said, "Wow, this is so beautiful. Thank you for letting me come."
>
> The old monk replied, "I didn't think you were ready. We'll try again next year."

Did you catch the young monk's mistake? Even though his remark was positive, it still represented his *egoic, thought-based judgment* of the experience as "beautiful." This comment betrayed the fact that he was still operating from the small self's perspective, walking through life not only thinking about but also *comparing* each moment to some ideal that his ego desired. Luckily for him, this one happened to fit the bill. Such activity in the mind promotes neither joy nor ataraxis and represents a primary cause of suffering. In contrast, the old monk was simply taking it all in and experiencing the sheer joy of being alive. For him, it didn't matter if he experienced sunshine or rain, mountains or plains, being alone or with another person; he was just happy to be out there. He was trying to show his young student, and us, how to be peaceful and happy as we walk through life.

ACTUALLY DO THIS

Let's try a new practice to help you experience a simple phenomenon without your sixth and seventh consciousnesses interfering. I want you to hum out loud, but allow your awareness to interact *directly* with the sound produced via the auditory (first) consciousness. *Do not* go to thought to know what you're doing or evaluate your performance. Just allow awareness to experience a moment of auditory consciousness without the mental and afflicted consciousnesses interfering. Drop all thoughts—no "I am now humming" or "This is dumb; I sound like an idiot" or "I don't think I'm getting the point of this." Just allow your awareness to experience the sound directly without interpretation or judgment. The only mistake you can make is trying too hard.

Try it a few times: "Hmmmmm…"

CHAPTER HIGHLIGHTS

Through the identification process, you came to believe you were an ego function—a small, inadequate, insecure, fragile, lonely being who thinks about themselves all day. What a shame, given that evolution only ever created the ego function to help you survive. You were never meant to live in the ego function (seventh consciousness) and its afflicted stories (sixth consciousness).

Key Insights

- The ego function evolved in the brain to keep us safe. But it defines and views itself (its perspective) as a mind floating around inside a body and therefore experiences core vulnerabilities such as inadequacy, insecurity/fragility, powerlessness, and loneliness, which are its traits.

- Seven types of consciousness deliver the phenomenal world you live in: the five sense consciousnesses, the mental consciousness, and the afflicted consciousness, which arises from the mind's identification with the ego function. All suffering occurs as a result of this identification. You become the ego function that is so self-concerned and terrified of the world. This is the perspective of the small self.

- The mind is not required to adopt the small self's perspective; instead, it can develop a Great Self perspective by dissolving the afflicted (seventh) consciousness, which fosters a healthy relationship to the mental (sixth) consciousness. This one shift in perspective represents a complete solution to the problem of the core vulnerabilities and all the anxiety, depression, addiction, rumination, and mindlessness they cause.

The Great Self represents a seismic identity shift compared to that of the small self. This shift occurs because the Great Self bases its identity on awareness and its associated enlightened *perspective, traits, and relationships*, which differ radically from the ego function-based identity of small self.

But before I teach you how to transition from small self to Great Self, I think it would be good to get to know this new identity and its traits. The next chapter introduces you to the "real" you, who has been hiding behind the defense mechanisms that arose to help you survive all the fear, hurt, stress, trauma, and anxiety that the small self experienced.

PART 2

DEVELOPING A SOLUTION

CHAPTER 3

RECOGNIZING THE IMMACULATE BEING THAT YOU ARE

> I began to question the idea of myself as a being in need of protection, indeed as something that could be protected. Nothing can protect us… It struck me as I wrote that I was utterly vulnerable to every other person, every other creature on Earth, and they were also vulnerable to me… I began to seek other ways of understanding the self that might be more useful than this shivering, weak thing we must shore up against the world.[13]
>
> — JENN SHAPLAND

Why do so many people feel as if they are this weak, shivering thing that must be shored up against the world? Because they are identifying with the ego function—a small self that is fragile, paranoid, and always on guard. Thus just as Ms. Shapland did, we also need to seek other ways of understanding the self that might be sounder.

Get excited! You're about to learn more about the Great Self—a more stably defined and even "real" you who isn't inadequate, insecure, powerless, lonely, or envious, let alone subject to the suffering of incessant craving and aversion. This chapter invites you to reimagine your identity by shedding the fragile, fear-driven perspective of the small self (See Figure 2.1) and embracing the limitless *capacity* of the Great Self (Figure 2.2).

UNSTABLE NOTIONS OF THE SMALL SELF

Because constructs are ideas being imputed onto conscious phenomena, it makes no logical sense to apply a singular, constant label to something that's continuously changing. Referring to the former example of tree maturation, this would imply that a seed, sprout, sapling, and mature tree are all the same thing. Yet despite its rational invalidity, applying a static label to a constantly changing phenomenon is precisely what we do with respect to the small self.

Your particular small self received a name, the label with which you identify continually throughout your life, even though the basis for this label (a human being) has not remained the same for an instant. Not only do you no longer physically resemble the newborn who received this name, but your personality—including your interests, habits, likes and dislikes, thought patterns, and emotions—has undoubtedly evolved and transformed dramatically throughout your life. The same goes for the ego function, which communicates its rapidly shifting fears and demands through the mental (sixth) consciousness. There's also no constancy in the more peripheral or extrinsic things you most likely identify with, such as your familial background, education, socioeconomic status and job, relationships, and roles such as spouse, parent, or friend.

> **ACTUALLY DO THIS**
>
> 1. Set a timer for five minutes.
> 2. Scan your entire body, and release any tension you find.
> 3. Close your eyes, and watch your thoughts rise without judgment.
>
> Notice how thoughts arise in and fade from consciousness without your control. Warning: This can be a little unsettling at first.

Now I'm not suggesting that all those things—your physical body, thoughts, emotions, ego function, personalities, and roles—aren't you *at all*. Remember that with all constructs, we aren't asserting that they don't exist. We're being careful and specific about *how* they exist—as a dualistic, relative idea imputed onto an open, undefinable, and more ultimate (as opposed to relative) reality. And because reality is ultimately an open field of potential, your mind is free to define itself however it chooses through the process of identification. That definition has profound consequences, because it can result in a skewed and grossly limited perspective that causes you to relate to phenomena in afflicted ways.

So as one of my Buddhist teachers is famous for saying, "Fabricate carefully." You're currently paying a heavy, tragic price for failing to construct yourself carefully, because no one has taught you an alternative way to *know* and *be* who you are. I'll correct this mistake by the end of this chapter.

STABLE NOTIONS OF THE GREAT SELF

If we want to define ourselves stably and sensibly, we'll need to look for aspects of ourselves that *aren't* changing. After decades of study, contemplation, and meditation, I have identified four aspects that meet the stability criterion.

- Omnipresent (present at all times, in all situations), awake, *aware*, and cognizant consciousness
- Love and compassion
- Equanimous fabrication
- Bliss

These four things have always been present, or never entirely absent, for even a second. Everything else appears to be in a constant state of change. Let's look at each of these aspects of the Great Self more closely.

THE OMNIPRESENT GREAT SELF: SELF AS AWARENESS

If you slow down and pay attention to the arising of thoughts in your mind (the exercise above, which I'm sure you didn't foolishly skip over), you'll notice they spontaneously emerge from seemingly nowhere. As a result, people often refer to themselves as the owner of their thoughts, as in "my thoughts." But who or what does "my" refer to in that phrase? It can only be the thing that's aware that a thought has arisen—your awareness. You can't rationally claim to be the thoughts themselves, because you can't control them. You have no idea what will arise next, nor can you control what it will be, because you can't think a thought before it's *thunk*.

And if you believe you can volitionally stop the thoughts from arising, meditate for a couple of hours and see how that goes. If you still think the same thing, consider what occurs when a song gets stuck in your head. How does this happen, and why can't you just make it stop immediately? This experience is even more mysterious in the case of a song you don't like.

If you own your thoughts and thereby control them, shouldn't you be able to flip a switch and be done with it?

It's hilarious that the ego function and mental consciousness even need to talk to you. As author and former chief business officer of Google Mo Gawdat points out, if the sixth and seventh consciousnesses were really you, why do they need to tell you what's on their minds? Wouldn't you already know? I know this can seem strange at first, but it's also a relief to realize that you don't need to listen to the self-absorbed, demanding, and paranoid machinations of out-of-control mental processes that aren't really you.

As such, you must change your relationship to thoughts by learning to disidentify with them for joy and ataraxis to arise.

> **GET THIS!**
> You are neither your thoughts nor the owner of them.

As an engineer, I participated in design reviews during which we would review circuit simulation results. During one such review, my boss and good friend Bob noticed a significant current spike when the device started—a surge that could potentially damage the device. The following interaction ensued.

> *Bob:* Uhhh, what's that spike of current at startup?
>
> *Engineer (shrugging):* Yeah, it does that.
>
> *Bob:* Well, engineers like you get paid lots of money to make it *not* do that. Please fix it, and we'll review it again.

"It does that" became a lighthearted joke whenever we saw errant behavior on a simulator or in the lab. I now think this is how we should all interact with the judgmental and paranoid cognitions of the afflicted (seventh) consciousness: Shrug (symbolically) and say to yourself "It does that."

From one perspective, awareness is the field within which all conscious content plays out, including so-called external phenomena. Everything going on "out there" is also going on "in here." (Picture me pointing to my head.) Otherwise, you wouldn't know the external world. As I suggested earlier, you can think of awareness as the screen upon which the movie of life plays out, with the physical object called "you" acting as one of the characters. Notice that you only have one screen, a single *field of experience*, and you don't know how big it is because you couldn't possibly have another to compare it to, which is the only way of talking about the size of anything.

As the space where phenomena play out, you could say awareness is a lot like physical space in that it's not a *thing* per se and is nearly impossible to define without referring back to itself (as in "space is the *space* within which everything happens"), yet it is fundamental to reality.

I remember coming out of a meditation session once and turning to my meditation partner (who also happens to be my wife Jami) saying, "I think awareness and space might be the same thing." I was on the right track, but there's a critical difference between the two: Awareness, unlike space, has the knowing quality of cognizance and the traits of loving-kindness and compassion that physical space does not exhibit.

RECOGNIZING THE GREAT SELF'S LOVE AND COMPASSION

At various points in my own therapy, studies, and meditations, others have urged me to deeply investigate what motivated me at my core. What truly drove my thoughts, speech, and actions? As a result, I became aware that love was behind everything I did. As a baby, I was trying to love myself and get my needs met; otherwise, I wouldn't have cried out when I was hungry, for example. As a young person, I tried to love myself and others by establishing relationships of various types and developing my intellect. As an adult, I've always attempted to love myself and others in myriad ways. I admit that it hasn't always gone well and has occasionally gone rather horribly. (Just ask my ex-wife!)

That happens because of ego function identification, the root confusion that causes love to warp into bizarrely limited versions of itself as expressed through self-absorption, hatred, blame, and conflict—the sources of all suffering that ever existed. I can explain everything about my behavior if I am a loving being in my core, but mountains of confusion often obscure my good heart. I cannot, however, explain much about my experience and behavior if I'm an afflicted being in my core and, therefore, only doing good in service to my evil nature.

When you observe the mess the world is in, it can be difficult to see that love is behind everything. The world looks the way it does because confusion, fear, and small-minded self-absorption obscure our essential nature of love. Self-absorption causes love to present in the world in incredibly limited and distorted ways. It might sound crazy, but maybe self-absorption is the real devil running amok on planet Earth.

For its sake, awareness, whether experienced as vast or localized, doesn't experience its objects as separate from itself, nor is it affected in any way by phenomena. Thus awareness appears to interact with all phenomena with love, compassion, and unbiased acceptance.

> **GET THIS!**
> As a result of its interconnected and integrated nature, awareness also expresses its traits of loving-kindness and compassion for all appearances.

The point is that love and compassion are functions or traits of awareness, not the ego function (which often confuses love and egoic attachment). The above-mentioned discussion implies a new understanding of suffering. When you act against yourself as love and compassion, you will suffer. Blame and revenge may taste sweet to the afflicted ego function but feel terrible to your good heart.

Whenever I experience anger, let alone unleash it on a target (usually someone I love), I know that the next morning's meditation session is going to involve some crying. That said, in such moments, I haven't acted against another as much as I've acted against my true nature, and that just sucks every time.

RECOGNIZING THE GREAT SELF AS AN EQUANIMOUS MENTAL FABRICATOR OF REALITY

The mind of the small self constantly creates stories about reality (as opposed to experiencing reality directly). In the last chapter, I discussed the various forms of consciousness that combine to make the human experience—*what it's like* to be a human. I also discussed how the mental (sixth) consciousness applies constructs to the various conscious phenomena and then builds the story of reality from there, including the story of "me" through the identification process. However, we need to extend these concepts a bit further to see how the mind fabricates reality from the ground up.

The best analogy I've heard comes from Dr. Bernardo Kastrup, PhD, PhD. Yes, he has dual doctorate degrees—in philosophy and computer engineering. He designed the advanced computing systems for the CERN particle collider. He says you need to imagine that you were born in a cockpit with no windows, but there are some gauges displaying, in a particular way, some of the data of some of the phenomena happening outside the plane.[14] Accordingly, as discussed in the previous chapter, your brain displays the experience of the color blue for you when the retinas are excited by 450-nanometer light. What you call "reality" is nothing more than what's on the dials along with an infinitely complex and concocted story about how information on the dials relates to other information on the dials.

As Dr. Kastrup points out, you have no real idea what's going on outside the plane, but you think you do, to the point where you believe that's what you're observing. You take the information on the dials at face value, assuming it accurately represents all that you are *not* measuring. But what if the person who programmed the dials in the cockpit erred in their calculations, or there was a short circuit in one or more dials? You would still accept whatever was displayed as reality, as you would have no other frame of reference. And if you measured different things outside the plane, as dolphins and bats do with their echolocation consciousness, or changed how the information is displayed (the dials), you would call that "reality."

As if that's not mind-bending enough, let's add one more element to form a complete picture. The preceding discussion builds on the idea that your brain acts as the central processor for information from the senses, much like a smartphone's CPU processes data from its sensors: the camera (eyes), microphone (ears), case temperature (skin), etc. This implies that the CPU ascertains a relatively objective picture of reality, even though it measures only a little slice of that reality, as mentioned.

Unfortunately, according to modern neuroscience, that's not an accurate description of what's happening in the human brain.

More accurately, the brain produces the whole experience in the first place based on what it predicts is happening now and going to happen next, all rooted in what it believes happened in the past, known as its "priors."[15] Furthermore, the same neurons that produce dream-based realities produce the experience you're having right now, the only difference being that the awake brain takes into account a little of what's going on in the world by measuring the error between what it believes the sensors *should be* measuring and what they're *actually* measuring. That's right—this is a dream of the brain's making, and it only adjusts that dream when it receives overwhelming data that contradicts what it's currently producing for you.

The predicted mental interpretation of sensory information is easy to experience directly, given how easy it is to mess with. For example, take a look at Adelson's same color illusion (named after neuroscientist Edward H. Adelson,[16] who originally developed it).

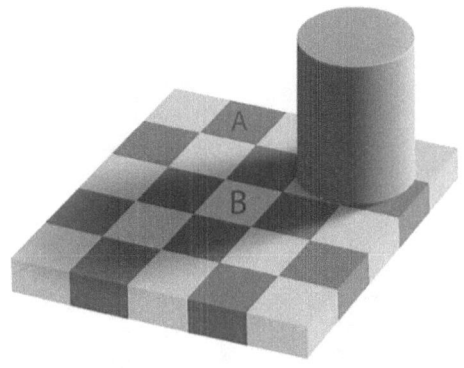

Figure 3.1 *The Adelson Same Color Illusion (Version 1)*[17]

If you didn't know better, you'd swear that it's an absolute fact of reality that boxes A and B are different shades of gray. But they aren't. I just checked the hex color codes for those two boxes, and they are both *objectively* #787878. That means the light entering the eyeballs from each box is the same wavelength, frequency, shade, or color (they all mean the same thing here). What's happening is that your brain, based on its priors when viewing other checkerboard-like patterns and shadows, isn't predicting them to be the same, so the hallucinatory experience it produces for awareness shows them to be different. Those two shades *are* identical, but you can't see them that way. This misperception implies that, due to your prior-based predictions, you cannot be *objective* but are instead *subjective*, even at the level of base perception. In other words, a different brain with different priors might present the shades as identical, but yours can't because it's hopelessly stuck in its priors.

Suppose I now add information that provides the brain with input indicating that its prediction is definitely wrong. In that case, you'll be better able to see the "truth" (but might continue to see some difference, albeit much less), as in this image.

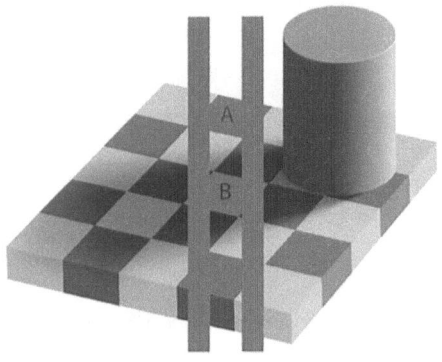

Figure 3.2 *The Adelson Same Color Illusion (Version 2)*[18]

GET THIS!
You aren't an objective observer of reality all the way down at the level of raw perception, because all perceptions are heavily influenced by the brain's priors.

This phenomenon isn't limited to vision; it involves all the senses. Numerous fascinating experiments reveal this, such as creating binaural beats with headphones, feeling an expected burning sensation despite no actual heat, and the excruciating pain a construction worker experiences when a nail pierces his boot, even though it entirely misses his foot.[19] This fact of reality has serious and far-reaching implications. If you can't be objective at the base level of perception, then any construction built from the objects of perception also hopelessly lacks objectivity.

To take this a step further, if you can't be objective at the base level of perception, how could you possibly be objective about the complex storyline derived from a multitude of those faulty perceptions? This is why I have a sign in my therapy office that states, "NO SUCH THING AS A TRUE STORY."

The deeper you go into the story, the further you move away from any kind of objective observation of external phenomena and the more deeply you enter your predictions. It appears as if natural selection fashioned consciousness to be helpful but not necessarily truthful. These theories all lead to one fantastic conclusion: What you have always referred to as "reality" does not represent what's *actually, objectively* going on. Instead, what you experience is merely a subjective version of reality based on subconscious predictions fueled by conscious or subconscious beliefs about what is happening.

Some might dismiss the concept of a fabricated reality as a new-age, woo-woo theory with no practical value, but nothing could be further from the truth. Anxiety, depression, and a bunch of other mental challenges have, as their basis, a mind that believes it is essentially a hopeless and powerless

> **GET THIS!**
>
> The ego function experiences itself as a victim of reality, but awareness experiences itself as an equanimous progenitor of reality and is no victim. It therefore rests in trait ataraxis.

victim of reality, which is simply false. Though it isn't a commonly used word, *equanimity* (think "equality" or "fairness") is a perfect descriptor of how awareness experiences phenomena, as it implies a trait of calmness and composure regardless of circumstances. Awareness simply isn't bothered in the slightest by anything; it can hold space for everything just by being itself.

The theory's implications extend beyond just the meaning you derive from your perceptions. Here's a typical exchange I have with depressed clients.

> *Joe:* What's happening right now that makes you unable to experience happiness?
>
> *Client:* I live a life of constant stress, exhaustion, conflict, and anxiety.
>
> *Joe:* Yeah, I know, but I mean right now. What's happening in this moment that's so bad?
>
> *Client:* Well, nothing.
>
> *Joe:* Then why aren't you happy right now, in this very moment?
>
> *Client:* I don't know. Aren't you supposed to be the one telling me that?

And tell them I do. The clients' lives have gone so poorly due to failed strategies and misdirected efforts to achieve happiness that their minds assume that this moment is also disappointing. They are stuck in their priors. Their minds are yet to see overwhelming contrary evidence and therefore produce the somatic and cognitive experience of depression. The same is true for anxiety and trauma (the most powerful of priors).

RECOGNIZING THE GREAT SELF'S BLISS

This one will be quick. The ego function views itself as small, isolated, fragile, insecure, and afraid—trapped in an endless cycle of craving and aversion. Thus it feels like a self-absorbed, anxious, and inadequate victim of reality. On the other hand, awareness experiences itself as the complete opposite: vast, integrated, indestructible, fearless, equanimous, and selfless, resting in constant, serene ataraxis.

What happens when the mind lets go of the ego's narrow perspective and all its afflicted stories and instead embraces the expansive view of awareness? Bliss. Sweet, gentle, perfect bliss. This isn't something newly created; it is and always has been present as an inherent trait of awareness. But it remains hidden as long as the mental (sixth) and afflicted (seventh) consciousnesses distort all experiences, as they incessantly do in the mind of the small self.

> **GET THIS!**
>
> Awareness is already blissfully resting in joy and ataraxis. All you must do is learn how to tap into this awareness to experience them.

COMPARISON OF THE SMALL SELF AND GREAT SELF

The shift in experience that results from the proposed shift in identity is seismic in nature. How you experience yourself and your life will be radically different depending on whether you are operating from a basis of hurt and fear or a basis of love and compassion. Let's hear from the small self and the Great Self about some of the ways they experience themselves and their respective realities (see Table 3.1 below).

ASPECT	SMALL SELF	GREAT SELF
Definition and boundaries	As others define me, I am a mind residing somewhere inside a body.	I define myself according to my direct experience, as a loving, compassionate, and cognizant awareness.
Relationship to danger	I am relatively easily harmed physically, psychologically, and emotionally.	While this body can be harmed and this brain may experience disturbance, I am indestructible.
Relationship to the world and others	I am separate from the world and others.	I am inextricably interconnected and interdependent with the world. I feel *with* others through compassion instead of apart from them.
Value	I am valued according to the way the world evaluates me, according to my speech, appearance, performance, and outcomes.	I am of inherent value that is incorruptible and eternal.
Relationship to the discerning aspect of the mind	I constantly compare myself to others in myriad ways and feel pride and shame as a result.	I see myself and others clearly without projecting or judging. Discernment functions without being contracted into the ego's judgmental voice against self or other.

ASPECT	SMALL SELF	GREAT SELF
Strategy for peace, happiness, and wellbeing	I focus on solving problems and finding peace and happiness through pleasure and by rearranging the external world, which causes chronic anxiety.	I respond spontaneously, appropriately, and skillfully, exhibiting confidence and ease instead of anxiety.
Primary motivations	I think, speak, and act primarily as a reaction to my fears and desires. I am obsessed with pleasure and pain, gain and loss, praise and blame, and fame and shame.	I think, speak, and act out of loving-kindness and compassion, equally applied to all appearances.
Relationship to ambition	I always feel as though I am "not quite there yet" and strive under a sense of incompleteness. I am a human doing instead of a human being.	I do whatever is needed without drama or burden. There is nothing I must do (other than be myself).
Relationship to the process of thinking	I think almost incessantly, which sustains my small-minded perspective.	I think when it's helpful to do so; otherwise, I rest in and enjoy the blissful and brilliant play of phenomena.

ASPECT	SMALL SELF	GREAT SELF
Relationship to the process of feeling and emoting	I project my own positive and negative feelings and emotions onto others and, in so doing, reify and reinforce my (small) self.	Feelings and emotions occur but are neither indulged nor rejected. They are more peripheral and do not command my sense of self.
Relationship to time	Due to incessant, fear-based thinking, I live primarily in the past or future.	I feel content and complete right now within an experience of timelessness. My attention is vividly present through nonjudgmental mindfulness, and the present feels boundless and complete in itself.
Relationship to reality	I am a victim of a reality that's happening to me.	I bask in the fearlessness and joy of the dance of all phenomena.

Table 3.1 Small Self vs. Great Self

As you now know, we want traits, not states. Another way of comparing the small self and Great Self is to look at the traits of their respective minds and how they relate to their lived experiences. Table 3.2 accomplishes just that.

TRAITS OF THE SMALL SELF'S MIND	TRAITS OF THE GREAT SELF'S MIND
Mindless	Mindful
Anxiety	Ataraxis
Incessant Rumination	Limited, Directed Thought
Tension/Stress	Calmness/Softness/Relaxation
Enslavement to Emotions	Volition/Emotional Freedom
Closed-Minded/Fixed Views	Open-Minded/Flexible Views
Judgmental	Accepting
Craving/Longing/Aversion/Dissatisfaction	Equanimity
Childish	Mature
Defensive	Open-Hearted/Vulnerable
Aggressive	Compassionate

Table 3.2 Traits of Mind: Small Self vs. Great Self

You can get a clear sense of the stark contrast between the experience of the small self and the Great Self, but language—a mere construct—cannot fully capture the full force of the Great Self experience. Direct experience transcends words, just as any description of what it's like to eat chocolate is nothing compared to the experience. It's not even a slight exaggeration to say they are different realities. Experientially, falling from Great Self back to small self feels like the equivalent of a world-class, elite athlete instantly becoming disabled.

Your mind is deeply conditioned to operate in small-self mode, so you might initially experience only brief glimpses of the Great Self. Ego function identification is some of the most intractable conditioning in the mind, which is why it's incredible that we can make progress at all. Luckily for us, the medicine is insanely more powerful than the disease. Once you learn to shift into the Great Self and do so frequently throughout the day, it puts a check on the small self's suffering, significantly reducing it and preventing things from getting out of hand. With continued daily cultivation, which you'll learn about in this book, the mind relaxes more and more into its new identity as the Great Self, and every year is then guaranteed to be better than the last, no matter what happens.

ACCEPTING JOY AND ATARAXIS AS YOUR BIRTHRIGHT

Joy arises from thinking, speaking, acting, and identifying with one's true nature as a loving, interconnected, interdependent, equanimous holder of awareness and powerful progenitor of reality. Unsurprisingly, suffering arises from thinking, speaking, and acting in opposition to one's true nature; in other words, identifying as a small, petty, fearful, isolated self that is a victim of reality.

Ataraxis arises from the equanimity of awareness, the patience it holds through its experience of timelessness, the love and compassion inherent in it for all beings, and the ethical behavior that naturally follows from these qualities.

Ultimate peace emerges when the mind, the fabricator of reality, stops perceiving that reality from a position of victimhood, thereby eradicating any potential for anxiety. *Dear reader, we have found a complete solution—a definition of ourselves that is stable, peaceful, and joyful regardless of circumstances.*

Awake, aware consciousness is the greatest thing in the universe, and your true self is the highest known expression of it. If you aren't getting goose bumps, or at least smiling, it's likely because this is still just another idea (or construct) for you and not a felt experience. That's no problem…we'll take care of that in Chapter 6.

How you act in accordance with your true identity as a cognizant conduit for love and compassion to enter the world will undoubtedly take on myriad different forms and roles based on your talents and interests. Still, you're really only ever doing that one thing—being yourself. For this being (labeled Joe), it doesn't matter if I'm working, helping my family, letting someone cut me off in traffic, or asking the grocery bagger how their day is going. I'm only doing one thing with one intention: cultivating the traits of a loving, compassionate, and overall healthy mind and heart by adjusting my perspective to align with my Great Self and crushing as much suffering as I can find along the way.

I'm so excited for you to define your own path in a similar way and integrate all aspects of your life accordingly.

The more you shift into your true identity, the more you will no longer be willing to play the foolish games you once played in your failed attempts at wellbeing. Although your life may look remarkably similar—a job, a partner, some friends, sporting activities, an occasional vacation, some healthy entertainment, and so on—the way you are internally going about your affairs and experiencing and relating to yourself and your reality will be indescribably different. Ataraxis will arise from knowing what you really are and what you're really doing here. Meaning and purpose will also arise quite easily. Your purpose is to move ever-closer to your great identity and away from your small one, and every experience is full of meaning as an element of that path.

I'll end this chapter by quoting my teacher Garchen Rinpoche,[20] a fully enlightened being (something he'd never admit to) who speaks only from the perspective of the Great Self. These words make the whole point of the first three chapters in a far more effective way than I possibly could have, no matter how many words I used. We need so many words because the statement below is simply too transcendental for us to fully grasp from the perspective of our confused, hurt, and scared small selves. Thus though the following is the only instruction we'll ever really need, it may require years, decades, and even lifetimes to fully realize and embody. Yes, it's *that* deep.

Now go tattoo this on your hand so you never lose sight of it.

> Love is the only cause of happiness.
> Its nature is all-pervasive, like space.
> Love is the sunlight of the mind.

CHAPTER HIGHLIGHTS

In this chapter, you learned to look deeply into notions of self to acquaint yourself with your Great Self. To arrive at a stable definition of the self and its perspective and traits, you must identify aspects that aren't changing over time.

Key Insights

Here are four things that appear to be stable.

- Awareness, primordial knowingness itself, is always present.

- Love and compassion are always the primary motivating forces, even when accidentally concentrated into a small point in time and space by the terrified ego function.

- The mind is always fabricating reality, all the way down to the base level of perception, as well as all the stories it weaves from those perceptions using constructs. Thus it's afraid of nothing and, therefore, naturally experiences equanimity and, as a result, ataraxis.

- The mind is naturally undisturbed, vast, integrated, indestructible, fearless, equanimous, and selfless, resting in the serene ataraxis in the reality it creates. This is blissful. Thus, identifying and resting as awareness represents a complete solution to the problem of suffering.

Joy and ataraxis, your birthright, are inherent traits of your mind. Thus you don't have to *do anything* to experience them; you simply have to *stop doing* the primary thing that prevents their exposure: the ego function identification of the afflicted (seventh) consciousness and the closely associated incessant paranoid rumination of the mental (sixth) consciousness. The more you accomplish that, the more the sunlight of the mind will shine forth in all its glory.

In the next chapter, you will discover how you can start changing habits that have prevented you from achieving your goals. There is no greater superpower than the ability to change anything you want about yourself and your life.

CHAPTER 4

LEARNING HOW TO CHANGE

> Watch your thoughts, they will become words.
> Watch your words, they will become actions.
> Watch your actions, they will become habits.
> Watch your habits, they will become character.
> Watch your character, it will become your destiny.
>
> — LAO TZU

The mind is a pattern-based machine that operates according to unconscious habits. Thus learning to program, deprogram, and reprogram the unconscious mind is the key skill you need to accomplish anything significant in life. Achieving joy/ataraxis and avoiding suffering will require that you diligently address habitual patterns of thought, speech, and action. More specifically, you must confront the deeply ingrained habit of acting against your true nature via pleasure chasing, pain avoidance, procrastination, and distraction seeking. One of my many teachers, Dzigar Kongtrul Rinpoche, literally wrote the book on diligence. In it, he states, "If we don't address our negative habits and tendencies, if we just lie there inert, ignoring them or in denial, our negativities will fester and grow bigger and bigger."[21]

This chapter may very well be the most impactful one in the book, because you can become anything you want if you learn how. It's just not easy. I've spent more hours than I care to admit trying to figure out why change is so difficult for us and which methods work best. The good news is that I've uncovered some effective techniques. The bad news is that I haven't found a way to change that doesn't involve discomfort. But as with all matters, pain can be minimized, and suffering can be eliminated.

In the next section, you'll learn how habits are formed and adjusted. This information will help you make changes to bring more joy into your life. Then I will teach you about two paths—developmental and fruitional—that you will use in the practices that follow.

UNDERSTANDING HOW HABITS ARE FORMED AND REINFORCED

Once you understand how habitual patterns form, you'll know how to unwind them. According to Buddhist psychology, the following three agents act in support of habit pattern *formation* and *reinforcement*.

- **Repetition:** The more you practice something (anything, really), the more it becomes grooved into your neural network, and the better you become at it.

- **Intensity:** The depth of the imprint made in the neural network will be proportional to the emotional intensity or intention you bring to whatever you're practicing.

- **Availability of the field:** The more opportunity you have to groove a pattern, the more you will tend to do so. This factor enables repetition to occur; that's how they're related.

In the West, Pulitzer Prize-winning author Charles Duhigg developed a different formulation that many have found highly beneficial.[22] He suggests that habits are formed and sustained according to the following sequence:

Cue/Trigger → Habitual Reaction → Reward

Example: Arrive home from work → Drink a glass of wine → Experience stress relief

To reconcile the two frameworks, consider how the three agents from the Buddhist framework operate behind the scenes of the three-step sequence from Charles Duhigg.

- *Availability of the field* relates to the presence of cues/triggers and all other contributing factors that enable the habitual reaction.

- *Intensity* relates to one's level of motivation behind the habitual reaction and the magnitude of the reward.

- *Repetition* is comprehended via the word *reaction*, as in re-action, and also relates to the frequency of practicing the entire sequence.

UNDERSTANDING HOW HABITS ARE ALTERED

In addition to its list of three factors contributing to habit formation and reinforcement, the Buddhist framework traditionally includes a fourth factor: *lack of a counteragent*. A counteragent is *anything* that resists a habit's formation or continuation. I initially found its inclusion in the list confusing, because the other three items are agents that *support* habit formation. I decided to call counteragents out separately here not only because it makes slightly more logical sense (to me) to do so, but also to emphasize the critical role they play in habit alteration. I find it reassuring to know that no habit can withstand an onslaught of skillfully developed and consistently applied counteragents.

As you'll see, the most potent counteragents bring the unconscious thoughts, beliefs, emotions, and behaviors fueling a particular habit pattern into consciousness in ways that are impossible to ignore. Counteragents can be classified according to the domain on which they operate, so I've broken them out into three main categories accordingly.

- **Cognitive** counteragents address thoughts and beliefs that motivate habits.

- **Emotional** counteragents address the emotions that motivate habits.

- **Behavioral** counteragents address the repetitive behaviors that keep habits in place.

COGNITIVE COUNTERAGENTS

Habits are initiated and reinforced according to your thoughts and beliefs. For example, if you want to be a high-performing athlete (a thought) and believe you're capable of becoming one, you will habituate the requisite behaviors that align with that outcome, such as eating a healthy diet, training consistently, and sleeping well.

One key cognitive element is intention, given how habitual behaviors directly follow from intentions. Problematic habit patterns can be exposed by seeing the conflicts between competing intentions. Continuing with the example, if the small-self you intends to use alcohol for daily stress relief, such an intention will run counter to the Great Self's higher one of becoming a high-performing athlete.

I've identified three flavors of highly effective cognitive counteragents.

- *Contemplation*, which involves bringing intention to your aspirations
- *Precommitment*, which requires that you decide ahead of time how you want to behave
- *Growth mindset*, which demands your sincere aspiration to be the type of person who strives for evolution

Contemplation: In the service of leading an examined life, it's time to take a hard look at how you're conducting yourself and why. Harmful habits like aggression and avoidance form unconsciously, so you must consciously and intentionally bring awareness to these patterns to dismantle them, and contemplation plays a vital role in the process.

Side Note: Mundane activities like showering and driving are great times to do contemplation work. If you're going to ruminate (which you are), you might as well make it productive!

> **GET THIS!**
> Contemplation enables you to make the unconscious conscious, as needed to alter unconscious patterns.

Successful contemplation leads to sound decision-making about who you want to be and how you want to conduct yourself. You can use the act of contemplation to emphasize your highest intentions and eliminate conflicting goals. The resulting clarity about where you are at and where you'd like to go will engender a powerful intention to change. It will help you understand the short-term and long-term costs and benefits of a particular habit and soundly delineate between the habits that support the aspirations of the Great Self and those that reinforce the fear-based and pleasure-seeking demands of the small self.

Precommitment: Once you've contemplated who you are and how you want to conduct yourself, it's time to make a solemn commitment and *write it down*. The adjective *solemn* here suggests that the first thing you must dedicate yourself to is taking your commitments seriously! It might be helpful to spend some time contemplating what caused you to fail to adhere to them in the past. Or maybe you need to understand why you can keep commitments made to others but not those you make to yourself. The goal is total, nonnegotiable, internal commitment.

Do you still need guilt and shame to hold you in place? It's okay if you do; it's better to work with what you've got than to complete no work at all! If you are this kind of person, one suggestion is to share your commitment with an accountability partner you trust not to weaponize it against you, especially when you slip up. Even more compelling is an accountability partner who's also making changes. And if you want to up the ante, define a friendly, moderate penalty each party will pay if either violates their commitment.

I once had a client commit to zero alcohol for 30 days while their accountability partner committed to zero marijuana for the same period. They also agreed that if either person broke their commitment, they would both have to restart the 30 days from the beginning! One person broke five days in, but the pain of having to make that phone call had the intended effect, and they both succeeded on their second try.

Growth Mindset: The growth mindset is one of those concepts that could've genuinely altered the entire course of my life had I been exposed to it in childhood. The basic idea is that your mindset determines an awful lot about how you approach and experience your life.

According to psychologist and mindset expert Dr. Carol Dweck, personal mindsets generally fall into two categories: fixed and growth.[23] The fixed mindset stems from the erroneous core belief that our identity and abilities are determined by unchangeable factors like genetics and everything that follows—talents, intelligence, personality, temperament, and moral character. Her and her team's research has proven that nothing could be further from the truth. Most people considered to be at the top of their profession did not ascend to that position without a consistent and gritty effort to develop themselves within the context of a growth mindset pushing from behind. Would you believe that Michael

Jordan was cut from his high school varsity basketball team? Can you imagine if he had given up?

Table 4.1 shows some of the characteristics of each mindset with respect to habit formation and alteration.

CATEGORY	FIXED MINDSET	GROWTH MINDSET
Power of the habitual mind	Victimized by it	Harnessed for good
Capabilities	Innate, static	Cultivated, developed
Effort	Pointless without immediate result	Critical to the long-term development of mastery
Challenging goals and efforts	To be avoided	To be sought
Failures	Taken personally as evidence of inadequacy	What's a failure? There are only opportunities!
Relationship to healthy pain and discomfort	Avoided at all costs	Fully embraced
Difficulties and hindrances	Opportunities to quit	Opportunities to grow and begin again

Table 4.1 Comparison of Fixed and Growth Mindsets

Cultivating a growth mindset involves stoking your imaginative and inspirational capacities. Find a role model you aim to exemplify, put their picture on your phone, and align your mindset with theirs by asking "How would they view this situation? How would they react?" Find inspirational passages that inspire you, and read them to yourself throughout the day. Envision through creative imagery what your life will be like, how you'll feel, and what your face will look like when you finally achieve the joy/ataraxis, discipline, and freedom from suffering.

EMOTIONAL COUNTERAGENTS

Subtle and not-so-subtle emotions drive our behaviors and can, therefore, serve as powerful counteragents. Continuing with the example of becoming a high-performing athlete, let's briefly look at how emotional counteragents support this aspiration.

Allowing your small self to drink alcohol in excess to relieve stress runs counter to your Great Self's aspiration. Here's the key: Acting against the Great Self is *always* painful. Conversely, when you're able to limit alcohol intake and instead use learned skills to work with stress, you feel pride from acting in concert with your highest aspirations, which feels amazing. You can only continue drinking if you focus your attention on the stress relief provided by alcohol and ignore the pain of acting against your true nature. The antidote then is to pay attention to the pain you're causing yourself and to the pleasurable feeling of pride when you're able to resist the urge to drink.

As you can see from the example, both negative emotions, which I refer to as *pain signals*, and positive emotions, which I refer to as *liberating signals*, can act as counteragents.

> **GET THIS!**
>
> Change is NOT about willpower; it's about paying attention to the right things.

Emotional mastery, the ability to experience pain without suffering, is perhaps the most impactful emotional counteragent. I'll briefly describe each of these below.

- **Pain Signals:** A pain signal counteragent reduces the intensity of an unwholesome emotional reward. (Remember: CUE → REACTION → REWARD.) When you experience an impulse to act against your highest aspirations, implementing a pain signal counteragent looks like consciously directing your attention to the painful feeling of *enslavement* and the suffering of guilt/shame you will experience by following through with the impulse. Doing so diverts your attention away from the desire-based thoughts about the pleasurable feeling you might temporarily experience by giving in to the impulse. In other words, *intentionally become increasingly familiar with the pain and suffering you're causing yourself*. Doing so cultivates a powerful counteragent against the behavior, simply because you don't want to feel bad!

    Adding pain signal counteragents can also be skillful. One way to do that is to consider how your behavior affects others by helping them experience pain and suffering. Get creative by adding some skillful (and even fun) pain signal counteragents of your own. For example, donating even a little money to your least favorite politician or political organization will likely set you straight pretty quickly. Trust me, it's *hard* to click that button!

    While pain signals can serve as powerful counteragents, they're also dangerous because they can be taken to an extreme that results in increased suffering through guilt and shame. We must avoid this outcome, because guilt and shame can severely damage self-confidence and self-efficacy, which will cause you to go backward.

ACTUALLY DO THIS

Pick one of your favorite bad habits that runs counter to your higher aspirations. Maybe it's as simple as eating junk food. Then go do it, but this time pay attention to what you're really doing to yourself and how you feel doing that.

How does it feel to eat junk and harm the precious body that supports your life?

How does it feel to know you are eating future belly fat and cancer?

I know it isn't pleasant, but you have to be willing to remove the reward for bad behavior if you want to change. I used to have a bit of an out-of-control sweet tooth, but a year of focusing on the fact that I was eating fat, diabetes, and cancer resolved it.

Slowly, over time, I came to view excessive added sugar as destructive and disgusting as it truly is.

- **Liberating Signals:** A liberating signal counteragent increases the intensity of a wholesome emotional reward. When you successfully act in accordance with your highest aspirations, consciously direct your attention to the resulting feelings of pride, confidence, and freedom. Doing so will divert your attention away from the unpleasant feelings that arise when foregoing immediate pleasure. And just as with pain signals, it can be helpful to develop additional liberating signals.

- **Emotional Mastery:** The more you master your emotions, the less they will master you. (I'll teach you how in Chapter 7.) Most importantly, you must learn to tolerate discomfort without it causing undue suffering of any kind, a trait I often refer to as *nontoxic hardness*. It's not the fake hardness of toxic masculinity that pretends things aren't painful when they actually are, but the full embrace of pain and discomfort as integral components of leading a disciplined life. To put it simply and bluntly, you need to develop hardness—thick skin within a deep acceptance that life is uncomfortable and even somewhat painful, every day, and nothing can ever change that.

> **GET THIS!**
> You're either going to get the productive, short-term hardship you choose or the unproductive, long-term hardship you don't, but there's no avoiding hardship in this life. There's no escape, so get over it already!

When you give in to the urge to avoid discomfort, you are telling yourself that you're weak and can't handle life. When you stay disciplined, you are telling yourself that you are strong and courageous. The best way to cultivate this counteragent is to do hard things every single day until pain and discomfort mean nothing to you other than an affirmation that you're on the right track.

BEHAVIORAL COUNTERAGENTS

Certain behaviors support or undermine habitual behaviors and can therefore serve as counteragents. For example, if you don't want to drink, you can stop being triggered into a purchase by finding another route home from work that avoids the liquor store. I've identified three types of behavioral counteragents:

- *Field availability reduction* means removing the triggers and resources needed to follow a habit.

- *Habitual reaction alteration* requires you to cultivate a different habitual response to the same cue/trigger.

- *Wholesome conflict* means cultivating conflicting priorities that counter the unwholesome habitual behavior.

Let's briefly explore each.

- **Field Availability Reduction:** There are two subcategories of possibilities when it comes to reducing the availability of the field. First, you can and should remove as many cues/triggers as possible. If driving by the liquor store triggers a purchase, find another way home. Second, whenever possible (given the circumstances), eliminate the resources that enable the unskillful reaction. If you want to stop eating potato chips, don't keep them in the house.

- **Habitual Reaction Alteration:** Programming an alternative reaction to a particular cue/trigger is a powerful counteragent against repeating the undesirable reaction. If you find yourself hitting snooze four times and missing your morning meditation or workout, stop allowing yourself to do that. Instead, set the alarm for when you actually need to get up, and as soon as you hear it, start moving your body. Force yourself to get out of bed without letting even two seconds pass—before your mind has the chance to spin up one of its clever justifications for staying under the warm covers. No thinking, debating, or negotiating—just program it in: alarm = movement.

Or maybe you have a drink every time you get home from work. In the morning, place your fresh workout clothes where you drop your work bag so that arriving home now means it's workout time. Don't even sit down, or you could be in real trouble when you feel the comfort of your recliner. Why do that to yourself? True warriors know the foolishness of fighting an unnecessary battle.

- **Wholesome Conflict:** We enable bad habits by making room for them in our lives. This category of counteragents reverses that by increasingly crowding out the bad behavior through intentional, wholesome conflict. The practice involves cultivating a new habitual behavior that directly conflicts with the one you're trying to change. If you want to stop smoking, start running and set a related goal, like completing a marathon in a year. And if that isn't enough, start competing. Eventually, the deleterious effects of smoking will interfere with your fitness. You'll eventually grow tired of training hard only to lose hard-won fitness for a brief moment of stress relief.

CHOOSING BETWEEN GRADUAL AND SUDDEN APPROACHES TO CHANGE

Before you commit to a change, you'll need to decide how you want to make it: gradually or suddenly (commonly known as "cold turkey"). Your particular combination of distress tolerance, neuroticism, and impulsivity (lack of executive functioning) will determine which approach works best for you.

For example, if you have a high tolerance for distress/discomfort, then by all means, quit the pattern cold turkey. If you tend toward impulsivity, a gradual approach may be more appropriate to avoid relapsing, which could cause you to become discouraged, regress, or even worse, give up altogether. If you're like me, you can immediately let go of some patterns, while others require extreme patience. The main thing is to set yourself up with *your* best chance of success and know that it is always okay to switch approaches and begin again if one is not working. The only thing that isn't okay is giving up entirely. It may take longer than you (and others) want, but if you can grit your teeth and stay on it by beginning again, change will come.

If you choose the cold-turkey approach, the counteragent tactics outlined in this chapter will still be beneficial before and during the attempt. For example, before your attempt, pay attention to the pattern's negative emotional consequences and contemplate what will happen if you refuse to change. During the attempt, concentrate throughout the day on how good it feels to be free and how proud of yourself you are.

For the gradual approach, the key is to start as small as necessary to strike a balance between progress and stress *while maintaining your commitment and momentum.* As long as some manageable stress and discomfort are present, the magnitude of the commitment simply doesn't matter. What does matter is the *consistent achievement of your goal.* You have to get in the habit of stacking wins. So if you find yourself violating a commitment more than about 10% of the time, you've likely set the bar too high.

I once had a client who had been drinking 24 beers a day for 17 years. I suggested he start by pouring out the last sip of beer number 24 every day for a month to get accustomed to making a commitment and stacking wins by denying himself something he wanted. It worked, and his reductions accelerated from there. When he arrived at what was for him an unsatisfying 12 beers a day around nine months later, he walked away entirely. I guess you could call his path a hybrid approach—gradual initially and sudden at the end.

I will say that a majority of my clients find 99% or less commitment more challenging than 100%. For example, let's say you commit to drink only one day per week. That means you face a somewhat grueling decision. Every day you have to determine whether today is the day. Containing yourself even further can help. Using the same example, precommitting to drink only on Saturday would take the daily decision-making away. But the pleasure you experience by drinking results in craving for Saturday and being disappointed that today isn't Saturday. Thus the intense and repeated experiences of craving and disappointment are powerful agents that support the habit.

The sudden approach is also not without its pitfalls and dangers. Most New Year's Eve resolutions die on the vine because the person tried to go from zero to hero overnight. For example, many people aspire to exercise more, so they hammer two hours a day in the gym, only to quit three weeks later because they stressed their body and mind far beyond their respective adaptive capacities. They didn't plan their attack with adequate respect for the habitual nature of their mind and got owned as a result. As a confused pleasure chaser, they also caused an imbalance in their pleasure/suffering equation that led to a decrease in their level of happiness.

In cases of severe alcohol or drug dependence, abruptly quitting can be hazardous and even deadly. Medically supervised detox may be necessary. Many legal psychotropic medications also require gradual tapering, so please be wise and compassionate toward yourself by getting educated and asking for help when necessary. Lastly, if you relapse after some time off, please be careful not to return to similar amounts you were using before the period of sobriety. We've lost hundreds of thousands of beautiful beings to this mistake.

TWO PATHS FORWARD

Now you understand your goals: You want joy and ataraxis. You understand how habits are formed and know how to cultivate counteragents that function as strategies to help you implement change. You understand approaches to change. This section teaches you about the developmental and fruitional approaches to the practices that you begin in the next chapter.

As a reminder, the goals are to cultivate the *traits* of joy and ataraxis while reducing suffering by developing new perspectives and ways of relating to them. To bring about that outcome, we will work with the following two approaches that readily present themselves.

- **Developmental Path:** This path requires that you develop the mental (sixth) and afflicted (seventh) consciousnesses to reduce the powerfully distracting fear and confusion they produce. I will refer to this as developmental path work. In Western psychology, the healthy ego function and associated mental processes resulting from such work is often referred to as the Healthy Adult in contrast to the Vulnerable Child (which results from ego function identification) and all its defenses.

- **Fruitional Path:** This approach helps you become increasingly familiar with *what it's like* to relax into your more authentic and stable identity as the Great Self, enabling you to enjoy the inherent joy and ataraxis already present in your mind. Borrowing from psychotherapist Bruce Tift's definition,[24] I will refer to this as fruitional path work. The word *fruitional* refers to the fact that these practices promote a stable identification with awareness through the direct realization of your true nature, which serves to replace ego function identification as your dominant operating mode.

The transformation process will include working with your mental (sixth) consciousness and afflicted (seventh) consciousness—aka your self-image, emotions, and behaviors.

Table 4.2 compares the developmental and fruitional paths.

ASPECT	DEVELOPMENTAL PATH	FRUITIONAL PATH
Mental (Sixth) Consciousness	Maintain realistic beliefs and associated expectations of self and other. Work skillfully with automatic thought content.	See through all mental stories by directly experiencing the fabricated nature of reality.
Afflicted (Seventh) Consciousness	Calm the ego function.	Transcend the ego function through non-identification.
Emotions	Cultivate emotional mastery and the confidence that you can handle anything.	Experience emotionality as wisdom.
Behaviors	Establish mindful self-control and exhibit increasingly disciplined, effective, and ethical behaviors.	Cultivate *naturally* skillful and ethical conduct in concert with your true identity as a loving and compassionate holder of awareness.

Table 4.2 Transforming Through Developmental and Fruitional Paths

Some of the practices in the following chapters are strictly developmental or fruitional, while others include elements of both. One benefit of including both approaches is that these strategies reinforce each other through positive feedback. As the afflicted (seventh) consciousness calms down, the mental (sixth) consciousness increasingly resolves its distorted thoughts and beliefs, creating steadier access to awareness and its beneficial qualities.

While you'll learn how to shift into higher levels of awareness, you'll notice that you're frequently (and frustratingly) yanked back into ego function identification by the paranoid ego function and its associated incessant talking and emoting. Thus the ego function needs to relax…a lot. But as the mind increasingly rests in awareness, awareness will hold and nurture the fragile, fear-based ego function—like the perfectly supportive parent the Vulnerable Child never had—offering the calming reassurance "I've got you, and we're okay." This further soothes and stabilizes the ego function. This process is how developmental and fruitional practices mutually reinforce each other and positive feedback is achieved.

> **GET THIS!**
> The developmental and fruitional paths mutually reinforce each other through positive feedback, so you must do both.

Remember that you're trying to shift the core desire for matters to be other than they are, and the honest truth is that healing and transformation take time and effort. Patience requires diligence based on a total internal commitment to change that makes your level of motivation irrelevant. Motivation comes and goes (like all emotions), so any challenging effort that relies on your level of motivation is likely doomed. It's why Navy SEAL and ultramarathoner David Goggins, one of the most disciplined and high-performing people on the planet, is famous for saying "Motivation is crap."[25] I'll discuss this and a few other challenges, along with their solutions, in the next chapter, but I wanted to bring this to your attention now to set proper expectations and avoid hindrances down the line.

I am compassionately trying to convey that your peace-and-happiness project is currently at its riskiest point. It's not that you won't see improvements and feel better in your daily life as a result of the practices I will be teaching you. Of course you will. It's just that early on, "feeling better" typically means achieving more positive mental *states*, and what you really want to achieve are lasting positive mental *traits*. If the experience of transitory positive mental *states* were ultimately satisfying, you wouldn't suffer so greatly when these states inevitably change. This is why you need to develop lasting *traits*, and it takes time to change how you feel in your core.

To supercharge your progress and ensure the maximum benefits from the work we're doing together, you have to commit yourself fully. I could bestow all the wisdom in the universe upon you, but it will remain as mere information unless you put in the effort to turn it into *your* wisdom. Knowledge becomes wisdom through experiential application. I am harping on this point because I know from experience (my own and that of my clients) that the ego will do everything it can to subvert this project. And because it has been with you forever, it knows the exact buttons to push to shut you down.

If I had to boil it down to just one thing I desperately want to convey to you, it is this: The traits and states of mind you desire are internal conditions (already within you—right there at your fingertips!), but they require increasing familiarization through cultivation. So get cultivating immediately, and never stop.

Once you learn the practices, performing the minimum set outlined in the following chapters requires about a minute every hour or two, for a total of 15

> **GET THIS!**
> You'll need to do work you won't want to do—work your ego function is scared to do—but there's no other way forward.

minutes a day, roughly 1.6% of your 16 waking hours. Thoroughly performing all the practices would require about 45 minutes total, approximately 4.7% of your day. It's not so overwhelming when you look at it this way, is it?

Actually ask yourself this question: Is 45 minutes per day dedicated to cultivating a lifetime of wellbeing too much to ask?

You've got this. Let's get to work.

CHAPTER HIGHLIGHTS

The mind constantly forms habits; the only question is whether this happens unconsciously or with conscious intention. Additionally, every counteragent that detracts from one habit could be considered an agent that supports another. From this perspective, the counteragents outlined in this chapter are the tactics you'll use to alter your brain's unconscious patterns.

Key Insights

- You can always cultivate positive and negative cognitive, emotional, and behavioral counteragents and envision a better future for yourself. It is also critical to determine which tactics are most effective for you and stick with those.

- Habits form from the combination of four factors: repetition, intensity, availability of the field, and lack of a counteragent.

- Changing habits isn't about willpower. It's about paying attention to the entire situation, becoming more familiar with each particular aspect of it, and successfully employing the appropriate counteragents. Thus the technique of directing your attention is the primary way you make the unconscious conscious.

- You always have the choice between short-term pleasure followed by longer-term suffering, including feelings of powerlessness, guilt, and shame…and short-term pain followed by longer-lasting joy/ataraxis and freedom. You won't always make the right choice, but when you falter, there's only one thing to do: Begin again. And again. And again. Never ever even consider giving up.

- Your path forward will include developmental practices that cultivate a Healthy Adult version of the ego function and fruitional practices that help the mind directly come to rest in its natural state of awareness. This promotes the shift in identity from small self to Great Self.

- Though the developmental and fruitional paths mutually reinforce each other through positive feedback, change takes time and will be slow in the beginning. Thus patience, trust, and above all diligence will be required.

The reward for your patience, trust, and diligence through this section of the book is coming next: the tried-and-true practices you can start today! I will begin by teaching you how to cultivate the most important component or basis of any path for transformation—joyful diligence.

PART 3

THE PRACTICES

CHAPTER 5

CULTIVATING JOYFUL DILIGENCE

> One can choose to go back toward safety or forward toward growth. Growth must be chosen again and again; fear must be overcome again and again.
>
> — ABRAHAM MASLOW

You'll need to muster a high level of diligence to succeed on any path of transformation. This chapter gives you the tools to develop this critical mental trait. Diligence is *the* key habit behind all major successes you will achieve in life. So the worst move you can make is to believe you don't need this initial cultivation phase. Trust me on this one: Though you may bring extreme discipline to particular areas of your life, self-transformational work differs for reasons I will discuss. Consequently, you'll need to set up a base of operations—an indestructible foundation upon which you'll build your castle. Going forward, you'll integrate this work into another practice, but for the next two weeks, concentrate primarily on developing these skills; otherwise, your castle will likely collapse during construction, and this engineer can't let that happen.

THE THREE TYPES OF LAZINESS

To fully prepare you, I want to introduce you to some of the most common conscious and unconscious habit patterns you'll need to work through to achieve your goals. Buddhist psychology defines *laziness* as any habitual pattern of thought or behavior that hinders the achievement of your Great Self's aspirations. Let's take a look at the various forms of laziness. The counteragent tactics mentioned in Chapter 4 are effective against all forms of laziness, but I'll mention specific ones that I've found particularly relevant and effective against each.

THE LAZINESS OF YEARNING FOR IDLENESS

This form of laziness represents your attachment to sleep, leisure, and general idleness. It specifically does not refer to your legitimate need for rest and recovery. It's more about that moment of being trapped under your bed's warm blankets or lying on the couch all day bingeing a television show—which you justifiably deserve, given the stressful week your ego function caused itself to have! Generally, it arises consciously; you know when you're giving in to it. Given how powerful this form of laziness can be, it does not need to hide in the shadows and prefers to come right at you. As such, this form of laziness must be attacked with counteragents daily and sometimes even hourly.

The best counteragents I've found for the laziness of yearning for rest are contemplation, precommitment, nontoxic hardness, and especially pain signals. It just doesn't feel good to lie around like a slug for very long once you start paying close attention to how you feel about your behavior in those moments.

THE LAZINESS OF DISTRACTION

This form of laziness represents your attachment to mundane activities, distractions, and the pleasures produced by both. A lot of circumstance management fits into this category, especially all the "busyness" in your life that steals invaluable seconds, minutes, and hours from what you find important. I put busyness in quotes because I am referring to the kind you create for yourself to avoid doing the things you don't want to do. I am *not* referring to the person working two jobs and attending night school while rearing five kids. That person *is* busy.

Your intense desire to avoid boredom—a state of mind representing a lack of present-moment engagement—also falls under this form of laziness. So-called doomscrolling represents modern life's latest innovation in this area, as if we needed a more powerful way of ignoring what's important to us. The problem is that indulging a craving only leads to more craving, given the ego function's insatiable nature, just as drinking saltwater leads to more thirst and eventual death.

This is why we advise crack addicts that the first thing they need to do is move out of the crack den. I've become convinced that this is the most challenging factor for us. We live in a comfortable "crack den" surrounded by other comfort addicts. Worse yet, this particular addiction is encouraged by a relentless marketing machine that lies in its promise that happiness is just one more purchase or distraction away.

The best counteragents for this are contemplation, precommitment, emotional mastery, and especially field availability reduction through the setting of strict limits. Implementation suggestion: Identify what you are avoiding through distraction, determine what you want your relationship to distraction to be going forward, commit to a limit, enact the limit, and skillfully but fearlessly face the emotions that result when you no longer distract yourself from the immediate experiences of your life. Face what you need to face, and deal with it.

THE LAZINESS OF SELF-DISPARAGEMENT

When the Dalai Lama first came to the West, he was shocked by the pervasiveness of self-doubt and self-hatred he encountered. Though many people are consciously aware of how much they doubt and/or hate themselves, this nasty little bugger loves to hide in unconscious shadows. This lack of self-esteem, self-confidence, self-efficacy, and self-empowerment permits us, as Kongtrul Rinpoche states, "to avoid having to rise to the occasion and do what needs to be done."[26] The best counteragents against the laziness of self-disparagement are contemplation that leads to a total internal commitment about who you are and how you want to be, a growth mindset that knows greatness is coming, and emotional mastery that puts you back in the driver's seat.

THE JOY OF DILIGENCE: NON-ARROGANT PRIDE

The best emotional counteragent against all forms of resistance to change, especially the laziness of self-disparagement, is non-arrogant pride. Arrogant pride is what ego functions do. It is temporary, self-absorbed, and often confused, given that the being is not responsible for the majority of factors that led to the success. Though it can be difficult, looking deeply into all the factors that led to success yields only one conclusion: We aren't nearly as responsible for our good fortune as our ego functions would like to believe.

Non-arrogant pride, however, is almost entirely different. When we align with our true nature, pride reveals and reflects the brilliance of our being like the sun breaking through the clouds. It is the joy of being ourselves in our highest expression. Its joy and bliss reflect the goodness of the totality of a situation as opposed to arrogant pride that takes pleasure in self-absorption.

Becoming more familiar with this experience is the greatest antidote to afflictive habitual behaviors that exists. It is *the* reward for being willing to experience short-term discomfort in service to your highest aspirations. It simply feels incredible to act in accordance with your highest aspirations. It is the reward for being diligent. You must get familiar with and even addicted to how good it feels.

There's nothing wrong with the fact that our minds become addicted; we just need to get them addicted to the right things! So get addicted to feeling amazing about yourself, and see where that takes you. In my experience, when I align with my Great Self, my mind seems to receive "permission" to be joyful. Thus non-arrogant pride is also the primary antidote to guilt and shame. At least it is for me, and I'd love to hear how you experience it.

WRAPPING UP DILIGENCE

At this point, I hope you're starting to see just how much stands in the way of your transformation. Your brain's predictive nature and learned helplessness make you fear change and doubt its possibility. Our brains simply aren't wired to prioritize growth leading to long-term, unknowable outcomes, especially if it is a challenging process. Time and again, our minds reach for more manageable, short-term, well-known outcomes, even those that deliver long-term disappointment and suffering. Evolution strikes again, paradoxically thwarting our continued evolution!

At this point, I also hope you're starting to realize that there is a viable way out of this mess. The fantastic news is that you have the most highly adaptable machine the universe has ever created on your shoulders. The odds are not against you; only a fixed mindset of self-disparagement creates that belief. If you commit wholeheartedly to the work, the odds aren't just in your favor. They're worth an all-in bet. So bet the farm, and accept that you're great.

I once had a coach tell me that I was afraid to be great. Man, I cried at that one. Still do. We're all great, if only we are brave enough to discover the source of greatness within us.

You're a human, so walk with some swagger and come and take what's yours.

YOUR FIRST PRACTICE: 14 DAYS TO DILIGENCE

Per the agents supporting habit formation, you have to perform these practices with *intentional intensity* for them to produce the intended effect. If you fail to, you're likely imprisoning yourself in afflicted patterns. So please love yourself enough by giving yourself a chance at authentic and stable wellbeing by fully engaging in the work.

You may find it helpful to record your outputs in a healing and transformation journal. I like to use an artificial intelligence-based tool to clean up my rambling stream of consciousness and format it nicely for my journal. If the day's exercise is *contemplation*, record the insights produced. If the day's exercise is *noticing*, record in your journal what it was like to notice that particular aspect of your experience.

Day 1 > Contemplation

- Am I really willing to engage in these practices for the next 14 days without my effort falling off as it has in the past?
- What kinds of things will hinder me, and how will I prevent them from doing so?
- Do I really want to change, and if so, what am I willing to do to make it happen?

Day 2 > Contemplation

Reflect on your activities for the past two weeks. Ask yourself:

- What am I doing with my days, and what do I aspire to do?
- What are the costs of staying right where I am?

Try the deathbed test: Imagine you're on your deathbed looking back at your life. What would that future self think about how you're conducting yourself today? What parts of your life would your future self wish you'd let go of sooner? This contemplation will produce the counteragent of friction in your mind—a tension between what your lazy ego function wants you to do and what your Great Self wants you to do. Becoming more *intensely familiar* with that friction will be key to altering habitual behaviors. You're sacrificing your future self for a moment of pleasure. Is that a trade you're willing to keep making for the rest of your life? When do you finally commit? Today is yesterday's tomorrow, so what will make tomorrow different?

Day 3 > Noticing and Contemplation

Today, engage in a time-wasting activity and notice how you feel during and after. Bring awareness to the fact that you're wasting your precious life and abandoning your higher aspirations, especially given that you have no idea how much time you have left to become who you're meant to be and truly live accordingly. Feel the pulls of desire and distraction and contemplate:

- What's happening to me right now? How does my Great Self feel about this?

Become familiar with this pain signal as intensely as possible, as it will represent a powerful counteragent.

Day 4 > Noticing

Today, intentionally resist the urge to engage in a time-wasting activity and do something good for yourself instead, no matter how small. Bring awareness to the joyful feelings of *pride* and *freedom* you experience and become familiar with them as intensely as possible. Similar to the pain signals that the Great Self experiences when you capitulate, these liberating emotions represent powerful counteragents.

Day 5 > Noticing

Engage in a habitual behavior that harms your body in some relatively minor way, such as eating junk food. Notice how you feel when you bring awareness to the fact that you're harming your most precious asset: the physical form awareness has taken to know and love the world and experience the sheer joy of conscious experience. You're hurting yourself at that moment, so notice what that's like and become familiar with this feeling as intensely as you can, as unpleasant as doing so may be. The disgust you might feel is a powerful counteragent. You want to stop doing it so often and intensely, don't you?

Day 6 > Noticing and Contemplation

Resist the urge to engage in a body-harming activity you would've normally done today and do something positive instead, like taking a walk. Again, notice the joyful feelings of pride and freedom that come from no longer being enslaved to a temporary moment of craving, and become familiar with this feeling as intensely as you can to cultivate this counteragent. During your healthy walk, contemplate:

- It's unpleasant to deny myself something I crave, but so what?
- Really, what's a little discomfort in service to my goal of finally being free of the destructive habits that have plagued my whole life?

- It's time to get over myself—it's just a bunch of temporary sensations anyway, so why do I care so much?
- How can I make discomfort increasingly irrelevant to me?

Hint: Do something uncomfortable every day, until discomfort means nothing to you anymore.[27] Paradoxically, the discipline of restriction *is* freedom.

Day 7 > Contemplation

- How do I typically stay distracted or otherwise avoid feeling my emotions, and which do I avoid most?

There are many emotions, so it may benefit you to refer to an emotion wheel or similar emotional inventory to provide the necessary language. A simple internet search will quickly produce what you need. Be as specific as possible.

Day 8 > Noticing and Contemplation

You're just past halfway in this exercise. Notice what working with your mind has been like over the past week. Then contemplate:

- Concerning this process I'm following, what have I struggled with most?
- What have I enjoyed most?
- How can I adjust my approach to help me enjoy working with my mind even more?
- Would it help to carve out a set time for this kind of work?

- Do I need to tell my loved ones what I'm trying to accomplish and ask for their support and encouragement?
- Do I need an accountability partner?

Day 9 > Noticing

Do something unexpected for someone else, preferably without them knowing. Engage and notice what it's like to be fully present with a moment of awareness while applying its innate virtue of compassion. Become more familiar with what it's like to be the good being that you are.

Day 10 > Contemplation

Consider the hardship you endured supporting a more significant and likely longer-term objective, such as learning a trade or earning a promotion. Also, reflect on the fact that everyone you've ever admired persevered through tremendous hardship in their quest for greatness. Then contemplate:

- What's really stopping me from accepting this basic fact of life—that all great things come from hardship, and nothing remarkable has ever been produced by laziness?
- Am I ready to finally grow up and accept life on life's terms?

Day 11 > Contemplation

Kongtrul Rinpoche states that self-confidence is derived from two sources: (1) knowing what you need to do and how to do it and

(2) understanding that nothing is static, especially the human mind.[28] Contemplate:

- Am I ready to fully accept that joy and ataraxis are my birthright?

- Many others, who started in a far worse state than I did, achieved these traits through consistent daily effort.

- Why would I ever think that the same isn't just possible but also *inevitable* for me?

Day 12 > Contemplation

During your more mundane activities, such as cleaning up after dinner or folding laundry, ask yourself:

- What would lead me to be joyful in a moment like this?

Hint: Craving being somewhere else or doing something else will lead to a disengaged mind, which always results in suffering.

Day 13 > Contemplation

- Who can I draw inspiration from during my journey to wellness?

- How can I bring them into my mind and heart *daily* to provide me the courage and diligence to continue striving, especially during challenging times?

- Who are the people in my life who will most support me?

- Who will most hinder me?

- Who's likely to be threatened or exposed by my increasing joy, ataraxis, and fulfillment?

- Who's on a similar mission?

- Do I need better friends, and where would I find such people?

Day 14 > Noticing and Contemplation

You've completed 14 days of work. Bring awareness to the joy of growth and knowing that you're on your way out of suffering, that each step you've taken is part of a much larger context called your life's mission: the cultivation of joy and ataraxis and all the wonderful things that will result from their stable presence. You must find joy in your path; otherwise, you won't follow it consistently. It's that simple.

Contemplate:

- What do I *really* want in this life?

- Who do I *really* want to be?

- Am I tired of giving in to the craving and aversion that thwart my higher aspirations?

- Am I really willing to pay attention to the right things and change as a result?

Resolve that you're done relentlessly chasing after pleasures and distractions. Such a way of life is ordinary, lame, and beneath your Great Self.

BONUS EXERCISE: Even if it takes you a day or three more, I'd love it if you could imagine yourself five years from now having fully mastered diligence and personal transformation and living a life of joy and ataraxis filled with great relationships. Write a letter from this future version of yourself to encourage your present self. What's it like to have accomplished all this? How do you feel? What wisdom could you share? When you struggle, which you will at times, pull the letter out and have your Great Self chat with your small self.

CHAPTER HIGHLIGHTS

Obviously, you'll need to keep cultivating diligence and never stop, lest unconscious laziness creep back into your mind. In addition, you have many bad habits that could use some healthy pressure. Going forward, you'll integrate this work into the coming Setting Intentions and Nurturing Reflection practice, which I'll present in Chapter 9, which you'll (hopefully) diligently complete for a few minutes every day. That practice strengthens your commitment to diligence, but we needed to jump-start the process, which was this practice's purpose.

Changing yourself is hard, if not impossible, when you ignore the right things and fail to become increasingly familiar with them. This problem has existed as long as beings have roamed the Earth. Animals remain trapped in unconscious, instinctual patterns, changing only when external forces shape their behavior through a process psychologists refer to as classical conditioning. But you're a human, so all you must do is intentionally employ the capabilities of your human mind; the situation will eventually resolve itself, no matter how intractable the habitual pattern may seem at first.

Key Insights

- You have learned about the concept of diligence to keep progressing on your path and how to identify the three types of laziness—idleness, distraction, and self-disparagement—all of which hinder forward progress.

- Counteragents (presented in Chapter 4) such as contemplation and precommitment help you stay on track.

- Non-arrogant pride is the best way to bolster yourself as you change.

- In short, pay attention and be diligent, and everything will work out (eventually)!

You now have the ability to determine who you want to be and how to diligently conduct yourself accordingly. Next, you'll discover how to shift your mind away from its small-self mentality and toward that of the Great Self. I hope you're excited, because as I mentioned in the Introduction, this shift is what Sam Harris refers to as "the most important thing I have ever been explicitly taught by another human being."

CHAPTER 6

LEARNING HOW TO BE

> Your mind is your instrument. Learn to be its master, not its slave.
>
> — REMEZ SASSON

We are not victims of our minds. As I have stated ad nauseam at this point, relating to your experiences from the perspective of the paranoid small self isn't that great and never could be. I will even go so far as to say that *no amount of ego function development will bring us all the way home.* This chapter is about finally discovering the part of your mind that doesn't suffer, and learning how to rest there consistently and compassionately. The fruitional, open-hearted awareness approach teaches that we cannot achieve complete, authentic, and lasting joy, ataraxis, or wellbeing by merely altering our beliefs, calming our thoughts, or building a healthy—but still ego-identified—adult mind that clings to itself for safety. These are all excellent and essential achievements, but they fall short on their own. You should view them as supportive practices that help you evolve, not end points in themselves.

My teacher and open-hearted awareness master, Erik Pema Kunsang, stated it perfectly.

> [Resting in open-hearted awareness] is the medicine to be taken regularly by anyone who is deeply tired of carrying the burden of existence that has all been so pointless with seemingly no end to the worries. For what? For what, really? Dualistic mind is basically uncomfortable; it's basic pain. It's tiresome, a drag, a hassle, to exist in a dualistic way. It is the thorn in your side that you can't locate and pull out. And we need to notice this in order to [become] fed up [with this way of being]. No more of this pointless agony; I want to be totally at ease, not just as a peak experience that we chase or purchase, but as a basic way of being—free, really at ease.

I've sat with that question (What is all this worrying really about?) for many hours since I heard him ask it. My conclusion: It's much ado about nothing. We have no idea what's happening outside Dr. Kastrup's plane, and all our worrying is based in the erroneous belief that we do. This implies that it's **game over** for anxiety and depression—we are advancing on the enemy of suffering!

Let's quickly cover a few of the more challenging concepts to ensure your sixth consciousness doesn't get hung up on them.

- **Nonconceptuality/Nonduality:** The term *nonconceptuality* means the mind has dropped all constructs—the lines it draws on raw conscious experience to create a story. When the mind draws a line on reality, a "dual" is created—this and that. Duals co-arise and therefore cannot be separated, much to our dismay. For example, as soon as the phenomenon of (dualistic) love arises, so does the pain of inevitable separation. Thus the mind gives rise to love and the pain of separation as a dual pair; they always emerge together, though the pain arrives later.

So *nondual* means the mind has dropped all lines, including the line between itself and the world, and between awareness as a subject perceiving a separate, so-called external reality. With all its paranoia, the small self cannot exist within a mind resting in the total open-mindedness and nonattachment of nonconceptuality/nonduality. Sometimes you'll hear teachers say that the intention is to rest in "nondual, nonconceptual awareness." Doing so results in ataraxis.

- **Meta-awareness or Awareness of Awareness:** Remember, I pointed out one important distinction between consciousness and awareness: Awareness can become aware of itself, even in the absence of conscious phenomena. Thus awareness of awareness is *the* critical step in all these practices. Your mind is always aware and remains so even when you're asleep, so you get awareness for free. However, you're usually unaware that you're aware.

In these practices, you will be working toward becoming fully aware that you're aware and stop forgetting it. Awareness of awareness is critical because once

> **GET THIS!**
> The mind cannot be unaware; it can only be unaware that it is aware. Let that sink in for a few seconds.

awareness becomes aware of itself, it becomes aware of—and increasingly familiar with—its traits of cognizance (knowingness), wisdom, interconnectedness, love, kindness, compassion, joy, and ataraxis. You can then operate from that basis instead of the afflicted ego function. This shift changes pretty much *everything*.

- **Local Awareness (vs. Attention):** Think of attention as the focusing aspect of the small self's mind—the mental (sixth) consciousness. When you're paying attention, you're essentially thinking of that thing and only that thing. Though concentration practices can help settle it down, you can forget ever stabilizing it entirely unless you have a dozen hours a day to dedicate to the project (and *never* read the news). Local awareness, in contrast, is the focusing aspect of vast, open, spacious awareness and *can* be stabilized more readily.

> **GET THIS!**
> The difference between attention and local awareness is the locations of subject and object. With attention, the subject is located somewhere in your head, likely behind your eyeballs, and the object of attention is somewhere else. With local awareness, however, the subject and object are co-located and, therefore, no longer separate.

Refer back to Figure 2.2 in Chapter 2. Notice how the diagram presents awareness in two modes: Open and Spacious at the bottom and Local as the small bubble in the center. Of course, it's all awareness, but you experience it in two distinct ways. Recognizing both modes can help you take meaningful steps toward awakening to your true nature.

EXPLORING THE LEVELS OF MIND/AWARENESS

A map can be helpful when venturing into a new territory. You begin with the everyday mind of the small self and travel toward your destination: glorious, immaculate, open-hearted awareness—the mind of the Great Self. Use Table 6.1 to help you orient.

LEVEL	AREA OF MIND	DESCRIPTION	BENEFIT
1	Everyday Mind	Thought-based, ego-identified	Familiar but claustrophobic and grossly limiting
2	Subtle Mind	Mindful witness	Awareness begins to unblend from phenomena, especially thoughts
3	Awake-Aware Mind	Nondual, formless, timeless	Direct contact with the open, natural state
4	Simultaneous Mind	Holding form + nonduality/nonconceptuality	Integration, functionality, spaciousness
5	Heart Mind	Embodied love and compassion	The awakened mind in action

Table 6.1 The Five Levels of Mind

Nondual meditation master Loch Kelly outlined a path to five levels of mind/awareness that can be achieved. They include a few stops along the way. I'll provide his descriptions[29] and a bit of helpful commentary for each.

- **Everyday mind** *is experienced as sense perceptions, thoughts, and emotions. Everyday mind looks from thoughts and ego functions to create ego-identification and a subject-versus-object dualistic split that obscures the subtler levels of mind. Everyday mind uses attention and self-awareness to focus.*

  This is the mind you already know, even if you don't know you know, as the small self. It's a bit of a claustrophobic torture chamber, and I doubt there's more to be said about Level 1 mind than I've already said. The issue is not that it exists, but that awareness has been allowed to collapse in on the thinking function (ideologically captured by the afflicted seventh consciousness) to the exclusion of nearly all else most of the time. This is why you feel like a thinker stuck in your head.

- **Subtle mind** *is experienced as the ability to step back from everyday mind and be located in mindful awareness, the meditator, or an observing ego. Subtle mind looks from a* [nonjudgmental] *mindful witness of thoughts, feelings, and sensations as the contents of our experience arise and pass. Subtle mind uses mindful awareness and subtle-body awareness to focus.*

  Level 2 is (hopefully) achieved with mindfulness meditation, and learning to shift into subtle mind can be an important step toward lessening the ordinary stress experienced by the everyday mind of Level 1. Achieving Level 2 mind is essential because you can't change anything by making the necessary gentle adjustments if you don't even know what's going on, which is what's usually happening at Level 1.

- **Awake-aware mind** *knows itself as timeless, formless, changeless, contentless, spacious awareness. Awake-aware mind looks from a big-sky witness of spacious awareness to see subtle mind and everyday mind as well as the world. Awake-aware mind is already here and aware by itself, so when we look from it, we are using effortless mindfulness.*

Level 3 is where, in my opinion, things really get interesting, as it represents a radically different way of experiencing reality. At Level 3, the mind has dropped all duality and conceptuality. Suffering is impossible in this state because there is no self experiencing an afflicted story. The key thing to understand is that, while you feel wonderful resting at this level, you can't operate, because the mind has no concepts with which to navigate the world. You couldn't go to the grocery store because you wouldn't know what the word *broccoli* even means. Staying here for too long could represent an advanced form of spiritual bypassing.

- **Simultaneous mind** *experiences ultimate reality and relative reality at the same time. The ocean of awake awareness experiences all energy and form as its own waves. We feel spacious and pervasive, boundless freedom, and awake awareness is embodied as an interconnected presence while being capable of perceiving each previous level of consciousness. Simultaneous mind looks from unity consciousness, where nondual awareness is knowing from within our consciousness while not becoming ego-identified.*

At this level, the mind has integrated relative and ultimate realities, so you can once again operate.

- **Heart mind** *is free of the location of any particular witnessing self. In this level of mind, we feel connected and protected, vulnerable and courageous, and motivated to create and relate. Heart mindfulness looks from our ground of being, which is now operating from open-hearted awareness, a wisdom-based loving intelligence that feels boundless, interconnected, and fully human.*

  This is the mind of enlightenment, the mind of the Great Self. Our boundless heart is now fully manifest and present in the world, which is a blissful way to be. As Loch describes, this level of mind represents a new way of being with yourself and your emotions. It dramatically enables the freeing of long-stored and often repressed emotional and psychological patterns, even traumatic ones. There will no longer be a need for any kind of defensive shell, given how open-hearted awareness is both completely vulnerable within its invulnerability and solidly courageous as a result.

While that all sounds wonderful, you'll likely experience these various levels of mind on a spectrum ranging from "Is that it?" to "Holy smokes, that's insane!" Many people experience both of these simultaneously. This apparent paradox shouldn't be much of a surprise within an experience of nonduality. Such an experience is likely to include everything all at once, which is yet another bizarre experience (at first). The only risk is that you will underestimate the value of what you experienced, so don't do that. Instead, contemplate the magnitude of the shift that becomes possible when you stop operating from the small self. Your actions will no longer stem from its inadequate attempts to avoid feeling bad.

Then the big, beautiful question becomes "What now?"

What will you do now that you aren't operating from a basis of fear, deficiency, incessant thinking, and avoidance?

Many of your activities may look the same on the outside, but your motivations will shift, your interpretations will change, your relationships to those actions will evolve, and the meaning you draw from them will deepen in profound ways. You will be in a new identity, life, and reality at that point.

The process of meditation (remember gom) is one of increasing familiarity with a particular perspective, experience, or state of consciousness. That's all you're doing—becoming familiar with *what it's like* to rest in various states of awareness—open and vast, localized, heartfelt. This allows you to enjoy the inherent properties of that state—its *traits*. As you become more familiar with a particular state of consciousness, you will find it ever-easier to readily shift into it and remain there even when the ego function is hurt, scared, sad, angry, jealous, or all five.

A NOTE ABOUT MINDFULNESS MEDITATION

You may have tried your hand at mindfulness meditation, which is also sometimes referred to as *calm abiding*. You might be surprised to find that I don't provide mindfulness meditation instruction in this book. The main reason is that I no longer find it the best place to start learning *how to be*. I've had too many clients report that it led to little more than becoming hyper-aware of how much their out-of-control minds are suffering! The issue, of course, is that they were meditating as the small self and marinating in all its afflicted stories accordingly, and that isn't pleasant without distractions to save them.

The meditations in this chapter present various *direct* paths to experiencing your true nature as awareness. This objective was made perfectly clear by Erik Pema Kunsang in a private talk he gave to his students, with the following instruction:

> We need to start where we are, getting used to settling in ourself. That requires reminding, otherwise it's so easy to look out through the five senses with the curiosity "What was that?" "Hey, I need to see that," or "That sound—what was that?"
>
> That attitude "What was that?" is an expression of ignorance—"I didn't know, so I need to look to find out. Which way do I look?"—outside of this fundamental state. That is a habit...a very strong habit. We look at the object rather than looking into the subject. Isn't that true? And when we look at the objects, there are millions—it's endless. When we look into the subject, yourself, your own nature, there are not millions, there's just one that we need to grow familiar with.

That's the whole point of the exercises in this chapter, getting to know the only first-person subject that has ever existed—awareness.

Now that all said, if you struggle with these open awareness practices due to an intensely busy mind, mindfulness meditation may help you achieve some initial quietude to provide a little space in which to operate. Your mind may be refusing to surrender to the present moment for even 5 or 10 seconds. If so, please do not fret, as this is relatively common.

> My website (www.UnbreakableInc.com) provides instructions for a basic mindfulness of breathing exercise, as well as some recorded meditations if you prefer to be guided. Of course, if you find my approach to mental health useful, feel free to join me in an exploration of the mind and heart in one of my workshops or retreats.

AVOIDING MISSTEPS, DETOURS, AND WARNINGS

Before I dive into what can trip you up, please remember: Awareness is your natural state, meaning it is there in its completeness no matter what. You cannot break or diminish it. You can only forget about it. There are a few ways to make resting in awareness more challenging for yourself, so let's cover them to help you steer clear of these pitfalls.

- **Trying Too Hard:** I often observe new practitioners simply trying too hard, attempting to overly perfect the craft. Trying too hard is a craving-based, chasing type of endeavor—the kind of effort ego functions like to make. The "do-er" in your mind wants to achieve these states, but it can't. Shifting into awareness doesn't require such effort, because awareness is the base or natural state of the mind. People accidentally stumble into various flavors of it frequently, such as walking in nature or entering a flow state while working or playing sports. Art in nearly any form often provides access to awareness, which helps explain why so many people find solace in it.

- **Figuring It Out:** The brain might try to learn these methods the way it has learned every other skill by going to the thinking mind to "figure out" what to do and assess performance. This is a dead end. This process is more about teaching the mind to relax into itself through a process more akin to unlearning than learning.

  One common criticism I hear about these methods is that they're missing detailed instructions on how to shift into higher states. If you've never golfed before but want to learn how, you'll need to build your skills by creating new neural pathways and meticulously refining those skills through many hours of practice. This is a very active process. Conversely, the process of learning to rest in higher levels of awareness doesn't require any such extensive skill cultivation. In fact, the task of learning to shift into and remain in a higher level of awareness is fundamentally one of *stopping* all the activities that prevent the mind from fully experiencing its true nature. When clients say, "I don't get it," I want to compassionately shout at them, "You can't *not* get it, because your mind is already doing it!"

- **Doubt:** Most doubt stems from believing you'll never "get it." (You're right, thinking mind of the small self, you won't.) When this arises in your mind, simply thank the doubting part for its assessment and let it know that it can relax.

  Past negative experiences with religion or spirituality often create another form of doubt. A few clients of mine have reacted to these practices as if they are religious, new-age woo-woo, or even feel "culty," as one client put it. These modes of mind—and the practices that reveal and cultivate them—aren't inherently spiritual or religious, even if they arose within specific traditions. Additionally, neuroscience and neuropsychology increasingly support these practices and the results they produce.[30]

THE PRACTICES

Category: Fruitional Path
Minimum Time Commitment: Five seconds (once you get the hang of it)
When: As often as possible

Hundreds of practices have been developed in religious and secular circles to help us shift into higher states of awareness. Religious traditions including Judaism, Christianity, Sufism, and Taoism include various practices that enable the experience of awake awareness. St. Francis of Assisi said, "What we are looking for is what is looking."

Of course, Hinduism and Buddhism are full of them. In the West, Douglas Harding and Richard Lang developed "The Headless Way" meditations, drawing inspiration from Zen Buddhism, Hindu Advaita Vedanta, and Western approaches. Loch Kelly has developed "The Way of Effortless Mindfulness," which includes practices adapted from powerful Tibetan Buddhist Dzogchen methods that readily shift the mind into open-hearted, spacious awareness. Some of the practices in this chapter are drawn directly from his work. Other teachers like Rupert Spira, Craig Hamilton, Stephen Bodian, Peter Fenner, Jeannie Zandi, Amoda Maa, Rob

Burbea, and Adam Chacksfield offer their own teachings and associated practices, and the list could go on for quite a bit longer.

The following two practices will require exactly what the label suggests—practice—to realize their benefits fully. Trying a few each day consistently will certainly do the trick.

> There are guided versions of these practices, during which I add some helpful commentary, available on my website www.UnbreakableInc.com.

PRACTICE: AWARENESS OF INTERNAL STABILITY

I developed this practice while sitting by the ocean. We deeply desire stability but haven't found it in external circumstances nor internal thoughts and emotions. Thus you must learn to find the place of stability within and increasingly familiarize your mind with it.

1. Sit somewhere where you can observe consistent movement in front of you. The ocean works well, but you can also use traffic, clouds, or wind passing through trees.

2. Direct your awareness to the visual field—the act of seeing itself that is happening all on its own. Allow awareness to interact *directly* with visual (second) consciousness without referring to thought (see Figure 2.2).

3. Suspending the thinking process for a few seconds, hold your breath while directing awareness to become aware of the knowing quality of mind that observes the shifting images in front of you but is *perfectly stable in*

its observation. Notice that both the act of observing and the direct knowing of what is observed are not altered in the slightest by the movement of the images. Try to make your awareness primary in the mind.

4. Now move your awareness to the hearing (first) consciousness. Again, notice that both the act of hearing and the direct knowing of what is heard (absent concepts) are not altered by the shifting sounds.

5. Lastly, move local awareness to the mental (sixth) consciousness. Notice that thoughts can arise and pass without having any effect on the knowing space within which they are occurring.

The point of this is to help you make contact with that place inside you that is stable and not affected by the dance of conscious phenomena. As you familiarize yourself with this internal stability, you might try applying it to the most challenging aspect of experience for humans: emotions. Notice the stability that remains even when the ego function is annoyed by another driver, for example. Increasingly allow your mind to identify as the stable entity that holds the dynamic play of all phenomena.

PRACTICE: SHIFTING FROM ATTENTION (LEVEL 1) TO LOCAL AWARENESS AND THEN TO OPEN, SPACIOUS AWARENESS (LEVEL 3)

The following five glimpse practices are taken with permission directly from Loch Kelly's book *Shift into Freedom*.[1] My clients and I have found this sequence to be one of the easiest ways to directly show the mind the difference between attention and local awareness. Once that is accomplished, local awareness is employed to experience open, spacious awareness (Level 3). I'll add some helpful commentary in a few places based on descriptions and pointers I've heard Loch say in various retreats and trainings I've attended. *Direct quotes from his book will be italicized* so you can differentiate between his instructions and my commentary.

> Note: Recorded versions of these glimpses are available on my website at www.UnbreakableInc.com.

Glimpse 1: Experience Attention

Take a moment right now to explore the experience of attention.

1. *Look at one of your hands. Now move that hand out of your vision, and bring your attention to that hand* [using only your mind]. *Try to continue applying your attention there for a short while.*

2. *What was your experience of attention like?*

   Initially, when you use attention to focus, you may feel that your head (where your brain and eyes are located) is your central place of perceiving. When you bring your attention to your hand, does it feel like 'you' are in your head, looking down at your hand? Or does it seem as if 'you' are shining a flashlight from your head to your hand? Or do you feel connected, as if a telephone cable is running from your head to your hand and sending signals back and forth? Do you feel how attention can wander? Are you able to feel that maintaining attention is actually a continuous process of remembering and forgetting?

The key thing to notice in this glimpse is that the subject (you) is in a different location than the object (in this case, your hand).

Glimpse 2: Experience Local Awareness

Now that you've experienced attention, let's see how local awareness differs. In order to experience local awareness, you need to unhook local awareness from thought and know your hand directly from within. Try this for yourself now.

1. *Unhook local awareness from thought, and let local awareness begin to move down through your neck and know your shoulder from within.* You don't need instruction on how to unhook; you just do it. Remember, don't try too hard and don't assess your performance; just practice.

2. *Slowly move local awareness like a knowing, invisible bubble down your arm into your elbow. Feel the awareness of space and sensation directly from within.*

3. *Continue to let local awareness move down your forearm until it feels your hand from within.*

4. *Experience this new type of knowing that is happening directly, from within your hand.*

5. *Notice that when awareness knows your hand from within, it does not refer to a mental image of your hand. It feels the space and aliveness of the sensations so there is not a clear boundary of inside and out.* Awareness has no need to go to thought to know the felt experience of the hand, because it knows directly. Feel that!

Notice the way in which awake awareness knows itself and your body through local awareness. Once local awareness has unhooked, thought is no longer the primary mode of knowing, yet thought is available as needed. If you do not reference a memory or image of your hand, your experience of your hand shifts into direct knowing. Direct knowing is spacious, alive, and much more fluid in feeling than attention.

It can be helpful to intentionally refer to an image of your body and hand to familiarize your mind with what it's like to go to thought and concepts to "know" or "figure out" what's going on. Imagine an image of your body and of your hand with fingers. Then switch back to local awareness, which knows the hand from within and has no need to refer to any such image.

The key aspect of this experience that is different from attention is noticing that with local awareness, subject and object are co-located in the same place (as opposed to attention where they're in different locations). Local awareness knows directly from within the object.

You've just experienced how local awareness moves from thinking in your head to being able to directly know from within your hand. Now you can begin to get a sense of the feeling of local awareness unhooking and moving to other senses. The important thing here is feeling how local awareness moves. This next series, Glimpse 3 through Glimpse 5, will give you step-by-step training to unhook local awareness and begin to feel how it moves to different levels of mind.

Glimpse 3: Coming Back to Your Senses

In this exercise, you'll feel how local awareness unhooks before it moves.

1. *As you look at this page, feel local awareness unhook from thinking about the words to seeing the printed words as objects being seen.*

2. *Next, unhook local awareness from seeing, and shift to hearing. Notice the dramatic difference in your experience resulting from this small shift of awareness: from seeing to hearing.*

3. *As local awareness shifts back from hearing to seeing, take your time and feel local awareness as it moves from one sense to the other.*

4. *Now local awareness unhooks from seeing and thinking, and feels down through your neck into your upper body.*

5. *Notice that local awareness within your body is not looking down from thought, nor is it looking up to thought in order to know.*

6. *What is it like when local awareness feels and knows both awareness and the alive sensations directly from within your upper body?*

7. *Let's do the previous six steps again when you're ready, using a different object. Before you move, say to yourself: 'Awareness is about to shift from thinking to seeing, then shift from seeing to hearing.' Then go slowly and feel the process of awareness moving as it tunes out of seeing and into hearing.*

In order to feel local awareness moving, you can take your time now: Pause, look up from reading, and experience the ability to shift local awareness intentionally. First, feel local awareness unhook from seeing and move to join with hearing.

Second, feel local awareness unhook from hearing and move down through your neck to know your body directly from within. Feel what it's like for awareness to come back to your senses and know directly, from within your body, without referring to thought.

Referring to Figure 2.2 in Chapter 2, you are learning to move the little bubble of local awareness between the various sense faculties or consciousnesses.

Glimpse 4: Awareness of Space

Note: I find it helpful to be outside for this glimpse and the next.

Local awareness is malleable: It can focus and join with one of the senses. In this next glimpse, local awareness can let go and move to be aware of objectless space.

1. *Unhook local awareness from thought, and let it focus on hearing the sounds coming to one of your ears.*

2. *Focus neither on who is hearing [nor] what is heard, just the sensation of hearing.*

3. *Notice how awareness is able to focus on the vibration of sound in this one small area.*

4. *Now unhook local awareness from hearing, and open to the space outside your body in which sound is coming and going.*

5. *Notice the movement of sounds through space, but then become interested in the objectless space through which the sounds are moving.*

6. *Notice the effects of awareness of space.*

Glimpse 5: Awareness of Awareness

In this next glimpse, local awareness moves to space and then discovers spacious awareness. Here, we will let awareness mingle with space and become aware of itself. When local awareness opens to spacious awareness, you can focus on spacious awareness within your body or go to the space outside your body. Because our senses are so oriented to the front of our bodies, it might be easier to discover spacious awareness on one side of your body or behind your body.

1. *Unhook local awareness from thought and have awareness focus on hearing the sounds coming to one of your ears.*

2. *Don't focus on who is hearing or what is heard, just the sensation of hearing.*

3. *Notice how local awareness is able to focus on the vibration of sound at one ear.*

4. *Just as local awareness can focus on a very small area, notice how local awareness can now open to be interested in the space in which sound is coming and going.*

5. *Rather than focusing on the movement of sounds through space, let local awareness rest in the open space.*

6. *Local awareness opens to space until it discovers that open space is aware.*

7. *Feel that local awareness is like an air bubble blending into thin air and mingling with the field of spacious awareness that is already aware.*

8. *Let awareness palpably know and feel itself, without looking to thought or sensation.*

9. *Stay with this contentless, timeless, boundless awareness itself. Remain undistracted, without effort.* Take as long as you need to get a feel for spacious awareness being aware of itself without any physical or mental references. It can be like tuning in to a radio station of pure awareness. Only the knowing from awake awareness can confirm when you're there.

10. *For a minute or two, relax into abiding as this field aware of itself without subject or object.* When you relax into your true nature as awareness, you are the field of experience itself, inseparable from any objects of awareness.

11. *Rest as awareness: [Rest] in the spacious field that is nonphysical, thought-free, timeless, boundless, contentless, yet fully alert and aware.*

12. *When awake awareness is primary, include everything and notice that you are aware of thoughts, feelings, and sensations from sky-like spacious awareness.*

Try this sequence one or two times a day for the next month (or more) until you can readily shift your mind from attention to local awareness and then to open, spacious awareness. Becoming increasingly familiar with what it's like to rest as open, spacious awareness is absolutely critical. Though I'm not providing explicit instructions promoting the achievement of Levels 4 or 5, they often arrive so easily that many people fall into them without making any effort whatsoever. You very well may have popped into one or both of them during one of these glimpses, especially Glimpse 5. The big jump that's being cultivated in this sequence is from Level 2 to 3, which changes everything, because suffering is impossible and ataraxis is guaranteed at Level 3.

CHAPTER HIGHLIGHTS

In this chapter, I've presented various methods to help you rest back into yourself—your true nature. In this relatively short space, I've presented techniques that often require entire books and/or hours of instruction. There is infinitely more when learning about your heart mind, exposing its true nature, and living from that place. My purpose here was to help you get a tiny peek into what's available in the world and help you become increasingly excited about the prospect of ending your suffering. You'll need to practice, practice, practice and even go on some retreats if you want to deepen your practice. I may be biased, but I don't think there's anything more important to do than this. It is *the* game-changer in terms of how you experience yourself and your life.

Key Insights

- You live in a state of everyday mind. Other levels of mind are available, and discovering them will ease your suffering and help you be a more disciplined and diligent person overall.

- With practice, you can readily shift into awareness and rest in an aware/awake state that, although you may not have known it, is always present.

- These states of mind are not something you work hard to understand. You don't actually need to understand any of the theory! If you simply learn to move out of your own way, they are available to you.

- Trying too hard, trying to understand, and experiencing doubt can block you from experiencing these peaceful states of mind. Interfering is one way the ego function attempts to retain the control it is afraid to relinquish.

You now understand how to shift your mind into what I hope becomes your new default mode of operation. As you stabilize this new way of being, you'll notice the ability of powerful emotions to instantly drag you back into the mind of the small self. In the next chapter, you will discover how to develop emotional mastery, which supports the increased stabilization of the Great Self, so that feelings no longer control your thoughts, speech, or actions.

CHAPTER 7

MASTERING YOUR EMOTIONS

> He who fears he shall suffer already suffers what he fears.
>
> — MICHEL DE MONTAIGNE

We don't fear situations; we fear how we will feel when they occur, because we're generally unskilled at feeling bad and hate doing so as a result. Emotions are nothing more than helpful survival mechanisms—mere information—but that's not how we relate to them. We ascribe importance to them due to identification, as in "I am sad." Consequently, we relate to negative emotions with aversion (hatred light) and fight against them through incessant prevention, elimination, and avoidance mechanisms.

Think about that: We hate the very things that protect us and guide us toward growth and transformation.

You wouldn't be reading this book if it weren't for negative emotions; they're the best teacher in existence. And since they're a part of us, hating emotions is akin to hating ourselves. In this chapter, you will learn that unskillful emoting entails not only hating them but also experiencing them as overwhelming and overpowering, unnecessarily hijacking your mind for minutes, hours, and even days. Then you'll learn why skillful emoting is vital to your well-being. This chapter introduces two practices—one developmental and one fruitional—to help you get control over your emotions so they don't control you.

FIGHTING EMOTIONS RESULTS IN DISASTER

This hatred-based war on emotions is unnecessary, because they typically arise and pass very quickly, usually within single-digit minutes. Take laughing, for example. You start convulsing, making weird hiccupping sounds as if you are experiencing a kind of seizure, and water squirts out of your eyes. Somehow, it's socially acceptable to do this in public, and despite having no idea what you're laughing at, others often share in your joy and start laughing themselves. Those bodily reactions indicate that you're allowing yourself to experience the emotion fully, which helps it subside. Actively resist it, such as when you try your utmost *not* to laugh at a fart in church, and the impulse to laugh grows out of control.

I find it fascinating that in those rare moments when we allow ourselves to cry, the same bodily reactions occur—convulsing, hiccupping sounds, and water squirting from the eyes. And just as with positive emotions, when we fight against allowing the body to process negative emotions the way evolution programmed it to, we suffer for much longer than necessary.

In addition to suffering through a painful emotion for an extended period, suffering arises due to repression and suppression of negative emotions, because all that energy has to go somewhere. The mind directs it into the body, which results in progressive forms of unconscious anxiety. The process starts with striated muscle tension in the shoulders, head/face, belly, and elsewhere. If that isn't entirely effective, the mind directs energy to the smooth muscles of the gastrointestinal (GI) tract, causing loss of appetite, upset stomach, functional vomiting, irritable bowel syndrome, and other GI-related conditions. If that doesn't work, you might be in for a panic attack.

Jamming the energy of an emotion into the body in these ways causes mental havoc as the left brain struggles to make sense of the disturbance and find a way to stop it. When the brain can't figure out a viable external solution, it continues trying, because that's all it knows to do. This rumination can be challenging to stop as long as the somatic root of tension remains. In other words, afflicted rumination is sometimes a symptom of an underlying, unaddressed, somatic condition.

In the next chapter, I emphasize the need to fully feel the emotion during the consequences step of the ABCDE tool for this very reason. If you don't allow your body to process the emotion, you can apply the ABCDE tool until the cows come home, yet you might not feel much relief.

To illustrate this critical point further, here's an example from a client interaction.

> **GET THIS!**
>
> Fighting against emotions contributes to suffering in the forms of elongation of the experience, unconscious anxiety, and afflicted rumination, all of which require powerful distractions to stop.

Joe: We've explored this situation and, as is the case so often in life, I just don't see a good door to walk through that allows you to avoid some pretty severe pain. Do you?

Client: Definitely not. So what am I supposed to do, ball up in the fetal position over in the corner?

Joe (said with confidence that he'll likely want to accept the challenge after a little pushback): If that's what you need to do, yes, but that requires a high level of bravery.

Client: Bravery? Being a crybaby requires bravery?

Joe: Brave people walk the harder path. Which do you think is harder: allowing yourself to feel this pain or to drink it away?

Client: Feeling it, obviously. But why would I take the harder path when I have an option to avoid it?

Joe: Well, first, because you aren't avoiding anything—you're merely pushing the energy somewhere else. Additionally, feeling it is only difficult while you develop emotional expertise. It'll never be pleasant, but that eventually won't matter. Once you accomplish mastery, there's no question as to the more arduous path.

Client: How do I learn to let myself feel?

Joe: Maybe you and I will slowly walk down that path together. Does that sound alright?

Client: You're going to cry along with me?

Joe: We've laughed and gotten angry together, haven't we? What's the difference?

Client: How the hell do you cry every day?

Joe: I *want* to do it, because that's how connection and healing occur. I don't suffer over it nor do I take it home with me. I'll teach you how, but I can't just give you instructions. That would be like trying to teach you how to ski without ever taking you to a mountain. The fetal position in the corner is a double black diamond run. We'll be starting on the green runs!

In short, you probably need to cry or skillfully rage about what's really bothering you to get it to stop bothering you. It's just fine if raging out is the move you need to make, as long as you don't violate another being's rights in the process. I find that attempting to snap off my bicycle's crank arms for 30 minutes works exceptionally well to dissipate negative energy while also strengthening my body and providing a delicious squirt of endogenous morphine—a win-win scenario.

I'm not suggesting that every emotion you have will come and go in mere minutes. Some experiences in life are just awful, such as grief when someone passes, and that pain is going to be in the room with you for a good while, maybe forever. Continuing the example, the pain of death represents one of love's negative aspects, making it impossible for ordinary humans to eliminate this suffering entirely. As soon as love arises, the pain of inevitable separation also arises, but it appears later.

So while you might cry for a few minutes every day for the rest of your life, you don't have to suffer over it by resisting the fundamental truth that life is full of pain. Will you allow that pain to overtake your mind and heart forever? Why is that necessary? Is that what your lost loved one would want for you?

> **GET THIS!**
> We cannot avoid pain in life, but we can avoid the suffering that results from resisting it.

From one perspective, we fight to keep our hearts from breaking. From another, our hearts are already broken, and we fight to avoid fully experiencing it. All the busyness of circumstance management and relentless engagement in distractions are in service to ensuring we don't experience the darkness. Heck, most of what we refer to as our personalities aren't much more than defensive complexes whose primary purposes are (unskillfully) getting our needs met and defending against fully experiencing how awful it feels when they aren't.

HOW YOU BENEFIT FROM SKILLFUL EMOTING

We don't just want to avoid suffering; we want joy and ataraxis. One of my therapist mentors, Diana Fosha, PhD, said it best.

> To live a full and connected life in the face of difficulty and even tragedy requires the capacity to feel and make use of our emotional experience. People disconnect from their emotional

experience because they are afraid of being overwhelmed, humiliated, or revealed as inadequate by the force of feelings, only to pay the price later in depression, isolation, and anxiety.

Disconnect from your emotions, and you disconnect from yourself, others, and your life, because being human means living a deeply emotional experience all day, every day. I also believe that statement is an excellent way of stating the overarching goal of most transformative paths, which is to live a full and connected life no matter what happens to you.

Another way of realizing the importance of skillful emoting is to recognize that all the world can do to you is help you feel emotions (notice I didn't say "make" you feel). Of course, it can and undoubtedly will someday kill you, but that's not relevant to this discussion, because the real concern is how you experience your life *before* you check out. While myriad things can kill you, emotions aren't one of them. Once you master your emotions, you become genuinely indomitable and courageous.

> **GET THIS!**
> Living an authentic human life requires experiencing the full range of human emotionality.

Contemplative types typically avoid using the word *control* for thoughts and emotions because they recognize that states of consciousness cannot be forced into or out of existence. You can, however, cultivate ataraxis and a sense of control by working with them skillfully.

EMOTIONAL MASTERY DEFINED

What does it mean to master your emotions? In his book *Already Free*, Bruce Tift[31] outlined the following stages:

1. **Recognition:** Becoming aware of your emotional experience psychologically and somatically as well as the story driving it

2. **Tolerance:** Allowing yourself to be whatever you are at any given moment

3. **Acceptance:** Dropping all resistance to the present experience

4. **Kindness:** Feeling more relaxed, confident, and willing to move toward the experience

5. **Welcoming:** Wanting to feel what you feel, not because you like it, but because it's your truth

6. **Committing:** Giving up the fantasy of a daily life without pain

7. **Loving:** Unconditionally integrating all emotional experiences into yourself and your life

I find it fascinating that acceptance is *only* listed at Stage 3 of 7! I suspect that's because we don't just want to stop suffering, we want joy/ataraxis. Recall from Table 4.1 in Chapter 4 that the developmental path includes cultivating emotional mastery that results in knowing you can handle anything. I believe the first four stages outlined above accomplish that. However, the fruitional path includes experiencing emotionality as *wisdom*, which requires more than mere acceptance and kindness. It requires total integration, as stated in Stage 7 above.

PRACTICE: DEVELOPMENTAL EMOTIONAL MASTERY

Category: Developmental Path
Minimum Time Commitment: A few minutes
When: Whenever you're experiencing a powerful emotion

What follows is a comprehensive framework for working with emotions. It will seem time-consuming and even a bit arduous initially, but it will become reflexive and easy with practice.

1. **Name it.** This can be more challenging than it seems initially, so you might search the internet for something called an "emotion wheel" or something similar to help you learn the language you will need. Or label the emotion something that enables you to harness its power or at least be less overtaken by it. For example, the nervousness you feel before performing can be renamed "performance adrenaline," which may positively influence how you experience it.[32]

2. **Ask for more of it.** You want to be able to investigate it, don't you? This move also plays a bit of a trick on your mind, for when you ask for more of it, you are opening to the experience instead of fighting against it, which is *the* critical move.

3. **Describe it.** Use third-person language to describe the feeling's mental and physical signature in as much detail as possible. For example:

   > "When worried, I can feel that breathing is shallow, tight, and uncomfortable, and the heart rate is elevated. The mind is ruminating with thoughts that feel pressured, and there is a desire to talk to someone about what is on the mind and heart."

   That is the physical and mental signature of worry. Notice I switched language and spoke about those phenomena in the third person—*the* heart rate, *the* mind—and not *my* heart rate or *my* mind. The word *I* was only used to refer to the thing that is aware of the phenomena—awareness. Describing somatic symptoms can be challenging, depending on how closed off to your body you've become over the years. While repression is relatively common, you might need some help to convince your brain that emotions are safe to experience, because they weren't at some point in your past. Therapy can help that immensely (assuming the therapist has achieved this ability).

4. **Scan through the body.** Scan part by part and identify tension or discomfort residing anywhere. Consciously relax that part of the body if you can. Rub muscles that are in tension. If you suspect a muscle is even 5% activated, intentionally tense it up and then release it; this will help it relax if it was only partially activated. Lastly, try placing your hand over an affected area and breathing into that area. (I don't need to teach you how to do that; just do it.)

5. **Take a 4–7–8 breath.** This engages the parasympathetic nervous system and helps the body and mind calm down.

6. **Investigate it.** Whatever emotionality is still present, ask yourself, "Where is the wisdom in this? Can I just get out of the way and allow it?" Of course you can handle it. You already are handling it. But ask anyway. Notice how it feels to ask yourself these questions. Then ask yourself, "What else am I feeling right now?"

   Our minds tend to fixate on a particular emotion to the complete exclusion of all others. We're never only feeling one thing, so bring mindfulness to the other emotions present. You'll be shocked to find that you can be peaceful and angry simultaneously, which is weird (at first). You can learn to be comfortable in discomfort, which is a superpower you want.

7. **Distract from it.** When all else fails and you're still being hijacked by emotional suffering, distract yourself and know that doing so is okay. Try not to use extremely unhealthy or addictive means. Meditation and exercise are two effective and healthy ways of working with powerful energies in the body. You tried to work with the emotion first, and that's beautiful; feel good about that, but don't sit in overwhelming suffering, as that's not compassionate to yourself.

If this process seems like a lot, it's because it is. As I mentioned, you'll need to practice until it becomes reflexive.

PRACTICE: FRUITIONAL EMOTIONAL MASTERY

Category: Fruitional Path

Minimum Time Commitment: A few minutes
When: Whenever you're experiencing a powerful emotion

The following sequence again derives from Loch Kelly's work. It starts with the most afflicted way to experience an emotion and ends with the most skillful and peaceful. The goal of the exercise is to experience an emotion without *being* the emotion. The instruction is to first call an emotion to mind. If one isn't already present, it might help to use your ego function's favorite afflictive emotion, and you may need to imagine a scenario that evokes it. Once the emotion is present, say each phrase to yourself to help you shift your mind to that level of experience.

Level 1 Mind

1. I am <emotion> about <situation>.
   In this step, the mind is fully identified with emotion and incorrectly believes the cause to be an external situation.

2. I am <emotion>.
   The mind remains fully identified with emotion but relaxes its story around it.

3. I feel <emotion>.
   The mind lessens identification with emotion by identifying as the one feeling it instead of the one being it—a step in the direction of Level 2 mind—and drops the story entirely.

Level 2 Mind

4. I am aware of feeling <emotion>.
   The mind is identified as local awareness holding no story.

5. I am aware of a part of me that feels <emotion>.

Locate that part.
Awareness is brought to the fact that the emotion is but one part of a larger experience.

6. I am aware of other parts of me that are not feeling <emotion>.
   Locate one or two of those parts in conjunction with the part feeling the emotion.
   Awareness is brought to various coexisting parts.

Level 3 Mind

7. I am aware of the awareness that is aware of itself—spacious, pervasive, and free of <emotion>.
   Awareness becomes aware of itself, and the emotion largely falls away.

Please be patient with yourself. Mastery is a gradual process that will not happen overnight. Like almost everything else worthwhile, mastering your emotions will take time. But there's growth all along the way. The more you learn to work with emotions, the less they will cause suffering, the more joy and ataraxis you'll experience, and the more self-discipline you'll bring to your daily life.

CHAPTER HIGHLIGHTS

Prior to the development of emotional mastery, you feel that emotions drive you, and you often avoid feeling them fully because your mental and emotional systems are afraid of being overwhelmed by them. Yet it is the acceptance of them that you need to really come to terms with—to feel them without suffering. You must stop being at war with yourself. You might experience resistance to facing your emotions, but to attain joy, that is what you will need to do.

Key Insights

- They're "just" emotions, and you have to get over them so that they stop ruling your life.

- Most emotions will arise and pass quickly, but only if allowed to.

- Fighting against emotions causes them to have profound longer-term consequences. Emotional suppression and repression are primary causal factors in the establishment of most addictions because the addicted mind (incorrectly) believes it has found a way to avoid them.

- Defenses and repression will prevent you from fully experiencing emotions.

- Living an authentic life with excellent relationships requires an ability to experience the full range of human emotionality.

- There are developmental and fruitional methods to work with emotions, and it's beneficial to master both, because you'll likely struggle to achieve complete integration using developmental methods alone.

In the next chapter, I'll teach you how to dive into the depths of your psyche to help you see and change the afflicted patterns that are at the root of your suffering. I'll teach you one of the most powerful methods of transformation adapted from one of today's gold standards of mental health treatment: cognitive behavior therapy.

CHAPTER 8

KNOWING THY (SMALL) SELF

> Until you make the unconscious conscious, it will direct your life, and you will call it fate.
>
> — CARL JUNG

As opposed to a medical approach to mental illness that might ask "What's wrong with you?" we clinical social workers tend to ask "What happened to you?" Let's quickly wind up the sequence of what happened to you (and all of us) to see how the powerfully transformative practice outlined herein will help you unwind the mess.

Ignorance of True Identity →
Core Vulnerability

In being conditioned to identify with our ego function, we lose sight of our true identity as awareness. This ignorance of our true nature/identity gives rise to the core vulnerabilities of aloneness, fragility/insecurity, powerlessness, and inadequacy.

Ignorance of True Identity → Core Vulnerability
→ **Experiential Confirmation of Core Vulnerability → Maladaptive Schema**

Our mistaken identity as the ego function now established, we enter the world as the Vulnerable Child and have a variety of experiences. According to Western psychology, our minds develop *schemas*, which are ways of perceiving and relating to ourselves and the world, just as a *schematic* defines a particular circuit and how it will interact with the world around it (including other circuits).[33]

Positive, healthy experiences lead to the development of *adaptive* schemas that help us thrive in the world. Conversely, negative experiences (especially traumas) that powerfully confirm our core vulnerabilities lead to the development of *maladaptive* schemas. In some sense, that is what trauma is—a powerful experiential confirmation that you are the vulnerable and largely helpless ego function. Appendix I contains a list of maladaptive schemas for your reference.

Ignorance of True Identity → Core Vulnerability
→ Experiential Confirmation of Core Vulnerability → Maladaptive Schema →
Maladaptive Defensive Schema Mode

In response to a particular maladaptive schema, our minds automatically and unconsciously develop a way to survive by shifting into a different operating mode. Maladaptive schema modes can be considered defensive patterns that arise in response to the suffering produced by maladaptive schemas. How does the mind determine which defensive mode to enact? It ingeniously tries all of them to see what works and what doesn't. All of this happens without your knowledge. Appendix II contains a list of maladaptive schema modes for your reference.

> Ignorance of True Identity → Core Vulnerability → Experiential Confirmation of Core Vulnerability → Maladaptive Schema → Maladaptive Defensive Schema Mode → **Maladaptive Beliefs, Distorted Thoughts, Afflictive Emotions, and Defense Mechanisms**

At this stage, the mental (sixth) consciousness maintains erroneous and dysfunctional beliefs about itself, others, the world, and how it should relate to all three. These beliefs and distorted thinking patterns produce additional afflictive emotions. In response, the schema mode employs maladaptive defense mechanisms that arise in the forms of thoughts and behaviors designed to "protect" you from further vulnerability. Appendix III contains a list of the most common maladaptive defense mechanisms for your reference.

If the entire sequence feels like an endless loop of distorted beliefs, troubling thoughts, painful emotions, and dysfunctional relational patterns feeding into more of the same, that's because it is. This cycle is a clear example of how suffering compounds on itself. Maladaptive schemas warp your perception of reality in hidden ways you can't fathom, and the erroneous core belief that you're a separate, objective observer of reality prevents you from seeing accurately.

Because these distorted patterns are so deeply ingrained, many of us need an unbiased, trustworthy person to pinpoint areas where our perceptions have become warped. Since most people are unaware of their distortions, it is often most beneficial to go through this process with a therapist (or similarly qualified mental health professional). Even when your blind spots are pointed out accurately and with compassionate care, they're not often easy to accept, because the schema is diabolically skillful. Depersonalizing it by asking "How would this schema perceive this situation?" can help you view it with a more open heart and mind.

If the way you imagine the schema would perceive the situation matches your perception of the situation, you likely have something worth taking a hard look at with the tool outlined herein. Core vulnerabilities trigger intense emotional pain (understatement of the century), and unskillful defensive responses to that pain create countless problems for you and those around you. The sad part is that the purest and most perfect protection against pain—your resilient, compassionate heart—also lies hidden behind those same defense mechanisms. So you'll need a way to bring the unconscious into awareness to break free. The ABCDE tool outlined in the following practice is designed to help you do just that.

PRACTICE: SCHEMA-INFORMED COGNITIVE BEHAVIOR THERAPY: ABCDE TOOL

Category: Developmental Path
Minimum Time Commitment: 10 minutes
When: Whenever you experience a powerful emotion or repetitive pattern of reactivity

ABCDE stands for activating event, beliefs, consequences, disputes, and envisioning. I'll introduce the tool by describing each element while taking you through an example of its use (in italics).

> For a blank template, visit my website at www.UnbreakableInc.com.

First, identify the emotions you are using with the ABCDE tool to address, just as you did with the developmental exercise in the last chapter. If you find naming a particular emotion a challenge, searching the internet for an emotion wheel or emotion inventory might help. It's perfectly fine to go with one of the primary categorical emotions of sadness, fear, anger, disgust, jealousy, or guilt/shame.

Emotions: Disappointment and Fear

Activating Event: What event seems to be the cause of your emotional distress? Keep it simple; one or two sentences are plenty.

Activating Event: The integrated circuit chip I designed has a defect and fails by blowing up under the exact condition it was supposed to protect against.

Beliefs: What beliefs do you maintain around the event? Here's where you'll need to put a hard hat on and go digging. You'll notice the list of beliefs becomes longer the more deeply you understand your schema patterns. This step is where you figure out what's *really* bothering you.

First, refer to Appendix I and identify which schema(s) has (have) most likely been triggered by the activating event. Next, identify what this particular schema believes about the self, others, and the world. Investigating beliefs that may be operating unconsciously but still obviously motivating your automatic thoughts, feelings, and behaviors is critical. For example, if being criticized for your appearance bothers you, there is an implied but largely unconscious belief that you are your body.

Schema: Defectiveness/Shame

Beliefs:

1. *I cannot handle this level of disappointment.*

2. *I am my mind, and by association, I am also everything my mind produces, such as this chip. If the chip is defective, so am I.*

3. *I am a failure. My career has been a failure, and all the hard work and sacrifice has been for nothing.*

4. *My work products determine my value, and this failure has dramatically diminished it.*

5. *This failure will have profound consequences, not the least of which will be a diminished professional reputation.*

This list could go on, but you get the idea.

Consequences: What are the emotional, physiological, mental, behavioral, and situational consequences of your belief system? Can you allow yourself to feel and experience the pain fully? Be sure to invoke the skills you learned in the last chapter. What automatic thoughts arise from the belief system outlined in Step 2? Note: These fall under the category of mental consequences.

Consequences: Panic attack including mental disorientation, time distortion, highly elevated heart rate, and shallow breath, followed by incessant rumination, worry, sleeplessness, loss of appetite, crying, and vomiting

Defenses: Start by referring to Appendix II to determine the schema mode and Appendix III to determine the defense mechanisms the mind deployed in its attempt to avoid experiencing the schema. Then name any behaviors you exhibited as a result. Identifying these patterns will help you recognize them in the future and take skillful action accordingly.

Schema Mode: Perfectionist Overcompensator

Defense Mechanisms: Compensation, Intellectualization

Behaviors: Working far too many hours, exhibiting extreme perfectionism (violence against the self)

Dispute: Here you intentionally invoke the Healthy Adult mode and dispute *each* afflicted belief listed in Step 2. If a belief is (or could be) true, you may not be able to dispute it directly, but you can and should dispute its impact. (See example below.) It may also be helpful to hypothetically ask the Vulnerable Child what they would need to be willing to drop their defenses and feel what they need to in order to heal.

Disputed Beliefs:

1. *Of course, I can handle this emotion; it's just a racing heart, rapid breathing, and a bunch of stupid thoughts that aren't true. I have skills now.*

2. *I am not my mind, my level of training or skill, or anything they produce. I'm a beautiful being who's trying my best to contribute positively to the world.*

3. *One event does not make a career, and the only people who never make mistakes or experience failure are those who aren't doing anything interesting. I'm here to push the envelope, so damn the consequences.*

4. *Outcomes do not determine my inherent value. My good mind and heart determine it, and they are doing their very best.*

5. *How do I have any idea whatsoever what the consequences will be? It's much more likely that my reputation will survive intact (which it did).*

Envision as a Healthy Adult: This last step might be the most critical to ensure that this activity will have a transformational effect. Use your powers of creative visualization and imagine yourself back in the activating event, but this time as a Healthy Adult. Imagine experiencing the event in a whole new way based on your revised belief system. For maximum benefit, it's vital to imagine every detail you can about the situation—the sights, sounds, and smells—all of it.

I allow myself to feel disappointment using the skillful emoting skills I've cultivated (see Chapter 7). I will remind myself that all problems yield to analysis and that I have everything I need to solve this issue. I see myself working on the problem diligently and asking for assistance from others as required. I rest in the knowledge that my value as a human being remains unchanged, regardless of the outcome. I will face the consequences of this failure and remind myself that life is an adventure to embrace.

Envision as the Great Self: Though the ABCDE practice is primarily a developmental tactic, this step adds an optional fruitional element. Chapter 6 introduced you to exercises that will increasingly, with practice, enable you to shift to higher levels of awareness. The point of those practices is to experience relief through a massive shift in identity and perspective. As you cultivate that ability, trying the envision step of the ABCDE process from a higher level of awareness can be beneficial. In so doing, you'll experience directly how a higher level of mind effectively frees you from your priors and enables an easier rewriting of the script.

I unhook local awareness from thinking and shift it to my heart center. Compassion arises spontaneously, and there is an immediate calming effect as the mind settles into nondual, open-hearted awareness that can see through all appearances, including the appearance of a small, fearful self that has failed. This awareness holds the child and lets him know that he's doing a fantastic job in life, and he best not fully buy into the ego function's story of life. The child cries and feels better, knowing he is good despite this setback.

Until now, you likely believed that activating events cause the resulting consequences. (This failure "made me" sad and fearful.) Hopefully, you now understand that it's actually beliefs that cause consequences. What's spooky to think about is that, given the mind's prediction-based fabrication of reality, the beliefs also contributed heavily to the conditions that brought about the activating events in the first place. Think about that one for a second (or a week) and rest in the magnificence of the mind's capabilities.

Don't be discouraged if this exercise takes a little while the first time or two you try it. Twenty minutes or more is not uncommon. But once you've gone through it a few times, you will likely notice consistent themes or patterns emerging. You'll be able to refer back to your completed ABCDEs and quickly arrive at the most critical and final step: envisioning the situation according to the new belief system. As you re-envision and re-experience yourself and the situation in a new way, you will rewire the schema malware that infiltrated your mind unnoticed. This exercise can be emotionally challenging, so your amygdala might declare an emergency and shut it down. Therefore, practicing patience and kindness toward yourself is of the utmost importance. If you start to feel overwhelmed at any point, put the practice aside and use your skills (especially from the last chapter) to regulate your emotions. Once again, a good therapist could help you if you don't want to do this work alone.

I'll close by letting you know the outcome of one of the most traumatizing events in my life. It took me three days to muster the courage to tell my boss David that the chip had failed its most crucial test. Drumroll, please…

He barely stopped typing long enough to reply, "It's power electronics. This stuff blows up all the time. You'll fix it." Not only was he entirely unfazed by what I considered a tremendous failure, he showed confidence in me that I didn't have in myself. And fix it I did (with the help of some really cool technologies and even cooler people).

It's still strange when I reflect on the months I spent in abject suffering that required medical intervention all over a story fabricated from utterly false beliefs. That's what maladaptive schemas can do. Yes, I have lived a blessed and relatively privileged life, but that didn't stop a damn schema mode from nearly killing me. These things are *that* powerful, so please do your work.

CHAPTER HIGHLIGHTS

In this chapter, you learned how to analyze and change the operation of your small self, which will help it calm down. Helping the small self relax not only allows for more joy and ataraxis, it also helps your mind rest as the Great Self, which obliterates suffering. When you don't recognize your true identity as the Great Self, you adopt maladaptive schemas, schema modes, and defense mechanisms to deal with problems and traumas.

Key Insights

- Your mind is heavily conditioned to identify with your ego function, the small self.

- You function in the world as the Vulnerable Child. This is why most people have only achieved the mental and emotional maturity of a teenager.

- Your true identity is one of awareness, which forms the basis of the Great Self. The Great Self arises when the consciousnesses, especially the mental (sixth) consciousness, are managed by awareness instead of the ego function. Your ego functions are also managed by your awareness.

- The ABCDE tool helps you identify maladaptive schemas, schema modes, and defense mechanisms. By bringing attention to them and writing a new story that you envision, you can release yourself from their tyranny.

In addition to investigating the deeply held challenging aspects of your mind and heart, you also need to set your intentions each day to point your mind in the direction you want it to go. You must stop leading an unexamined and unintentional life. The next practice, setting intentions and nurturing reflection accomplishes that.

CHAPTER 9

SETTING INTENTIONS AND NURTURING REFLECTION

> The unexamined life is not worth living.
>
> — SOCRATES

One of the first things you're taught as a mountain biker is to *look where you want to go, not where you don't*. In other words, direct your attention where you intend to go. If you genuinely desire to head in the direction of emotional freedom, you must stop living unconsciously, mindlessly, and unintentionally and instead live a closely examined and directed life. Major problems often start out as small problems that were ignored for far too long. Burnout often occurs over the course of years as the nightly drink to "take the edge off" of stress insidiously becomes ever-less effective. Many divorces (including my own) were caused by a rift that formed as a tiny hairline fracture when no one was looking but then developed into a chasm before any remediating moves were made.

It sounds almost painfully obvious to say we need to direct our minds and lives, yet we don't—not on a daily basis as needed, anyway. But there's no other way forward, because if nothing changes, nothing changes—and nothing will change if we aren't even aware that it needs to.

I hope you're starting to see that the whole game of life is one of internal cultivation. This makes perfect sense, given that the quality of your life will be almost entirely determined by the quality of your mind. Prior to reading this book, directing your mind toward your higher aspirations throughout the day was most likely the number one thing you *weren't* doing.

My mother always said to me, "People don't change," and she was largely correct, but it's not because we can't. It's because we weren't taught *why* or *how* to constantly evolve—we weren't given *direction*.

EXPLORING THE ROLE OF ETHICS

The Dhammapada, a sacred text in Buddhism, states:

> Mind precedes all things; mind is their chief, mind-made are they. If one speaks or acts with an impure mind, suffering follows like the wheel of the cart follows the foot of the ox. If one speaks or acts with a pure mind, happiness follows like a shadow that never departs.

This passage articulates a basic formulation of the law of karmic cause and effect: *This* directly follows from *that*. Now karma can be a rather complicated topic, but you don't need to understand it as deeply as a monk or nun might to benefit immensely from the theory.

Given that the word *karma* has made its way into pop culture, I'd like to first discuss what it *isn't*. Karma is not a magical universal force that causes you to crash your car tomorrow because you intentionally killed a bug today. It's more that mental states condition the mind to experience more of the same. Simply put, *like begets like* and *practice makes perfect*. As I've discussed at length, thinking, speaking, and acting from the perspective of the small self and its self-absorbed tendencies conditions the mind to do more of that. This conditioning occurs because the mind is practicing a behavior and will get better at it because the brain—for better or for worse—improves at whatever it's allowed to do.

Let's look at an example to see how karma really works. Say you and I form a friendship based on trust and mutual respect. I then ask you to lend me $1,000, which you do, but I don't pay you back and, most importantly, never intended to. From my perspective, it would appear as if something good (me getting $1,000) came from something bad (the intentional act of stealing), but that's not what happened. The effect of receiving $1,000 didn't result from the cause of stealing; it resulted from the established bond of friendship.

The theory of karma suggests that the stealing of money is a cause for a negative result that hasn't shown up yet. But it will, in some other place and time. How? Well, if I'm so self-absorbed that I'm willing to manipulate and steal from a friend in this way, what kind of intimate relationship do you think I'm capable of maintaining? Through practice, the act of deceiving my friend further amplified my self-absorbed corruption, which will be one causal factor among many in my divorce eight years later (hypothetically speaking). But by then, the cause and effect will have become so separated in space and time that I likely won't put the two together. I won't be thinking, *I shouldn't have stolen that money, because now I'm in a messy divorce that's going to cost me many thousands of dollars*—but that's exactly what I should be thinking, because that's how it happened.

Or maybe I didn't get divorced, but my level of self-absorption led to depression and excessive drinking, which led to a DUI charge, which then cost me thousands of dollars. So if you think the negative act of stealing led to the positive result of the $1,000 staying in my bank account, go ask a friend how much divorce or a DUI costs. The point is that the result can occur in an infinite number of ways, but it *is* coming one way or another.

The law of karmic cause and effect suggests *it's the mind that essentially gets back at itself.* This is not to suggest that a part of your mind actively schemes against other parts; that's not what's happening. It's that everything is a cause for another result, and that result is unavoidable unless a concrete action is taken to avert it. It's not that complicated of an idea: How your mind responds to a given situation conditions it to respond in a similar way in the future. Thus no one gets away with anything, which is comforting to know. There is no need to take revenge on those who harm us; their minds will do our dirty work for us. Every selfish thought, word, or action *will* have a negative result in the mind—period, full stop, can't be any other way. Every indulged craving leads to more craving. Every healthy hardship intentionally avoided leads to weakness.

Ethical principles fall into the categories of thought, speech, and behavior. I've found it's easiest to start with gross behaviors first, such as "I intend to be more patient during my commutes today and not use my car to retaliate if someone cuts me off in traffic."

Setting Intentions and Nurturing Reflection

After you clean up your conduct a bit, try cultivating skillful speech next, such as "I will not flip the bird (a nonverbal communication) to anyone when they cut me off in traffic today." Then as you increasingly clean up your behavior and speech, start to work on your thoughts, as in...

I will not think terrible things about the person who cuts me off today. Instead, I will remember that they're a confused and suffering being as I once was and will wish them well on their way.

I will remember that the solicitors interrupting my book writing time are just doing their job and probably stress over money just as I do. They're trying to make a sale and don't intend to annoy me.

The idea is to move from gross to subtle and slowly clean up, or *purify*, your mind stream. You need to do this, because you cannot do harm in the world and expect joy and ataraxis to result. In that passage from the Dhammapada, I suspect purity means thinking, speaking, and acting in accordance with the Great Self, just as impurity implies acting from the small self.

The skillful approach to change is to keep it simple by picking one thing at a time that you're willing and motivated to address. Start small. The aspect of yourself that you're changing doesn't have to be a deeply ingrained part of your personality. The point is to do something, anything really, to keep your momentum and commitment to evolution fresh in your mind. You'll be shocked at what happens over time as you slowly change into the person you were always meant to be and experience the inherent joy and ataraxis that arise from doing so.

PRACTICE: SETTING DAILY INTENTIONS AND REFLECTIONS

Category: Developmental Path
Minimum Time Commitment: 10 minutes
When: Every day, morning and evening

The practice is simple. In the morning, you're going to carefully set your intentions and aspirations for the day. In the evening, you'll review your day to see how you did and make any necessary course corrections.

MORNING INTENTIONS

Spend about one minute on each step, making sure you fully embody the intention before starting your day.

1. **Cultivate diligence.** Remember from the practice 14 Days to Diligence outlined in Chapter 5, it's vital that you keep the positive pressure on your neurotic, habitual tendencies to engage the various forms of laziness. The practice is to pick one of the contemplation or noticing activities from Chapter 5 and work with it today. Or take the healing and growth bull by the horns by developing one of your own. You know what you need to work on. If not, just look at what bothers you on a regular basis. Ask yourself…

    - What would be good for me to contemplate?
    - What do I need to pay more attention to today?

    Becoming more familiar with how amazing it feels to act in concert with your Great Self is always a great option.

Now let me assure you, this is one practice that's really easy to blow off. Don't do that. You know where you lack diligence and discipline, so address it even if that means allowing yourself to *feel* what it's like to realize that you aren't being who you want to be or doing what you aspire to do. Think for 10 seconds about how nothing good will come from continuing to avoid the work of change. Yes, even this small action will have a positive result.

2. **Set your intention.** Pick *one habitual thing* to work on at a time, such as an ethical principle you're cultivating or a relationship you're improving. My clients often find it beneficial to work on lying (to others and themselves) and deception first. Bring that change to mind and determine how you will take a small, actionable step forward today. Then really commit to it with as powerful a heartfelt intention as you can.

    How are you going to be a part of the solution to our broken society today? How are you going to bring people together? How are you going to make life better for yourself and everyone around you? How will you direct your mind toward gratitude and positivity and away from its deeply habitual tendency to focus on the negative aspects of life?

3. **Don your armor.** The first two steps directed you toward positive changes you'd like to cultivate. But remember that your refined goals were not only the cultivation of joy/ataraxis, but also the avoidance of suffering. This step is meant to address that aspect of life. The practice is to ask yourself: What or who is most likely to disturb my mind today, and how do I intend to meet the challenge?

For example, "I will remind myself ten times today that my job is nothing more than a job that I choose to do for now, and someday I'll make a different choice." Maybe you exposed an erroneous core belief from some ABCDE work you've done, leading to something along the lines of "I will not cave to my feelings of inadequacy today. I'm going to walk with confidence into that meeting with the CEO and deliver the difficult message that I believe the time has come to exit the business."

4. **Anything else?** How else are you going to work with your mind today? You know what you need to work on, so add it here. The point is to get moving and stay moving.

EVENING REFLECTIONS

Unless you have something that requires a deeper exploration, these exercises will require between 30 seconds and two minutes each.

1. **Review your conduct.** How did you cultivate the thing you're working on this week? What stopped you, and how will you prevent it from stopping you again tomorrow? How did you speak and behave in general today? Is there anything that needs to be addressed? If you fell down, intelligently regret it without guilt or shame and reset your intention to do better tomorrow. Give someone an apology. Let your coworker know that despite yesterday's criticism, you really value them and their work.

   I think it's generally a mistake to turn this into a time-consuming activity. I just want you to think for 30 seconds about who you've been today, how you conducted yourself, and what you can do better tomorrow. You'll be shocked at the power of this small act.

2. **Assess the battle.** *What* disturbed your mind most today, *why* did it get to you, *what* did you try to do about it, and *what adjustments* do you need to make? Was your mind open to a new perspective, or was it stuck in habitual perceptions and meaning-making? Do you need to do an ABCDE on something?

3. **Cultivate gratitude.** This is one of those practices that I blew off for years despite it being suggested to me by therapists and Buddhist teachers alike. Boy, was that a mistake. Buddhist teachers are really good at kindly smacking you across the face when you need it.

I once let a teacher of mine know that I was feeling a high degree of stress. After a few more questions to better understand my situation, he replied, "You've been doing gratitude practice for over a year, haven't you? I guess it hasn't started to take root just yet. You might consider doubling your effort or figure out how your approach is flawed, given how unproductive it is." Ouch. But of course he was correct.

There may be no more foolish move than failing to direct your mind toward positivity as a counteragent against the ego function's habitual negativity. Again, being joyful will entail spending more time in joy and less time in judgment, worry, stress, and frustration.

I believe one reason gratitude and positive psychology in general work as well as they do is because they capitalize on the predictive nature of the brain. It's not a problem that your brain is a prediction machine, but you have to help it predict good things so that it produces the psychosomatic experiences of joy, contentment, and abundance.

The practice is simple: Think about a few things you're grateful for today, and don't use the same thing twice for a few months. Yes, you read that correctly. No duplicates for a few months. You might have to start looking for things to be thankful for throughout your day, which would be a wonderful thing to spend mental energy on. The most important thing, as always, is to *feel* what gratitude is like inside the mind and body. No feeling, no healing.

4. **Anything else?** If you added an element in the morning, review it here.

That's it for this practice. Leading an examined and intentionally directed life will help you avoid many problems. Better yet, doing so will guarantee that every year is better than the last. What more do you want out of life than for it to get better every year?

CHAPTER HIGHLIGHTS

In this chapter, you learned about karma and its effects on your life experience. Clarifying your intentions and paying attention to ethics is necessary to move toward a joyful existence. To put it simply, you can't do harm in the world by acting against your Great Self and expect joy and ataraxis to result. It's impossible. This chapter introduced a simple practice you can use to assess your progress.

Key Insights

- Karma is not a magical force. It is the result of the decisions you make and the reactions you cultivate.

- Being an ethical human being is necessary for happiness.

- Setting your intentions and reflecting on your performance daily can help you make course corrections and be in better touch with yourself.

Chapters 6 through 9 taught you practices that you will use to intentionally and powerfully cultivate your mind. While such formal work is critical, you must also respect the habitual nature of the mind that makes change a challenge.

In the next chapter, I'll show you how to break up your habitual patterns throughout the day, which will greatly accelerate the changes you want to see in your mind, heart, and life. You must turn the mind again, and again, and yet again—all day, every day! This is how change occurs: You cultivate a certain *state* and then return to it repeatedly until it becomes a *trait*.

CHAPTER 10

CHECKING AND RENEWING

> Small disciplines repeated with consistency every day lead to great achievements gained slowly over time.
>
> — JOHN C. MAXWELL

Despite lasting a minimum of 30 seconds and likely no more than two minutes, Check and Renew is by far the most important and life-altering tactic in the book. This is the one practice you don't want to drop. Your mind currently lives under the tyranny of mindless, habitual perspectives and associated reactions, and this will need to change immediately. The sixth and seventh consciousnesses simply cannot be allowed to operate mindlessly for hours on end without *supervision* and *intervention*. The afflicted (seventh) consciousness is like a little kid playing with matches, and they will burn the house down, often when you least expect it. Thus checking in with the mind and shifting it to a new perspective and relationship to that perspective throughout the day will be your main practice. Being a hybrid practice, it will include developmental and fruitional elements.

The practice is to check in with your mind and turn it in the direction you want it to go, and to do so frequently throughout the day. And by "frequently" I mean as often as your life circumstances can support. Every 15 minutes would be amazing, but that's not realistic for most people. Every two hours is the bare minimum, because once the trains (patterns) of affliction get rolling for hours, they can be hard to stop, let alone reverse.

PRACTICE: CHECK AND RENEW

Category: Hybrid
Minimum Time: 30 seconds
When: As often as possible

1. **Know what's up.** Snap into the present moment and query (a) your present state of mind and (b) the present traits of mind based on how you're relating to the present moment. Check and immediately address the following traits:

    - Resting in mindful, attentive presence versus mindless, distracted absence
    - Closed and fixed-minded versus open and flexible—the growth mindset
    - Resistant and defended versus accepting and vulnerable

2. **Relax your body and mind.** Take a 4–7–8 breath and SNAP into radical acceptance, noting how you feel at the end of the sequence. Generate a moment of total open-mindedness, and surrender to the present-moment experience, no matter how unpleasant it might be. Stop

resisting your experience of life. Doing so is causing you to suffer.

3. **Address emotions.** Bring love and attention to the body and mind by querying the dominant emotion present. Use the skills you've learned to address it cognitively and somatically if necessary. If you need to, conduct a brief ABCDE on the emotion to identify whatever defensive mode you might be in, and shift out of it.

4. **Adjust behavior.** Calling to mind this morning's intentions, ask yourself, "What is most skillful for the Healthy Adult to be speaking and doing in this moment?" and compare it to what you're doing. Adjust speech and behavior accordingly. Also, reflect for a second: How have you spoken and acted since your last Check and Renew? If you have anything to adjust, go fix it and be proud of yourself for doing so.

5. **Anything else?** Insert whatever you want in this step. Take charge of your path by getting creative; don't wait to be told how to heal your mind. You know what you need to do, so do it. Examples could be calling to mind an ethical principle you're cultivating such as honesty or a behavioral intention such as getting off your phone. Check in and adjust as necessary.

6. **Shift into the Great Self.** Shift into as high a state of awareness as you're capable of, noting what it's like to be in that state in contrast to the state you entered this Check and Renew with. Become aware of awareness's traits by bringing the soft, calm, stable, and loving presence that you are from the background to the foreground

in your mind. Feel non-neurotic, non-arrogant pride in the person you are and are becoming.

7. **Mindfully return.** Return to your activity from this state, making a gentle effort to maintain open, spacious awareness for as long as possible. Find joy through *full and total engagement* in whatever you are doing, no matter what it is, by focusing on the joy of conscious experience itself. Life is a crazy adventure full of ups and downs, so you might as well live it fully. What's the alternative?

Eventually and with practice, you'll be able to complete this step in less than a minute, unless you're under the spell of something difficult and need to take time to address it more thoroughly.

That's it for this exercise. If it doesn't seem like too much, that's because it isn't. Yet it will be *the* practice that alters your experience of life more quickly than any other. Without this step, the more formal practices you've learned in this book—learning how to be and acting from a place of love and compassion (Great Self) instead of hurt and fear (small self), mastering your emotions, cultivating a healthier version of your ego function, and leading an examined life—will not become unconsciously habitual, and you will not experience nearly as much change as you intend.

So turn the mind—again and again and again—until it gets the memo that the time for mindlessness has come to an end. No more immature, unchecked reactions. No more mindless, habitual behaviors and reactions. No more incessant, judgment-based rumination that steals the joy from every moment. Those are for immature, undeveloped minds, not for a mind like the one you are cultivating. Each moment is now full of meaning and purpose. Such behaviors are beneath you now, so walk with some swagger.

I'm proud of you, and I want you to be proud of yourself.

CHAPTER HIGHLIGHTS

In this chapter, you've learned how to take the fruits of your more formal practices into your daily life, which greatly accelerates their stabilization.

Key Insights

The process includes the following:

- Becoming aware of your current state
- Relaxing your body and mind
- Addressing powerful emotions that may have arisen since your last check
- Adjusting your conduct accordingly
- Shifting into the Great Self to help stabilize this way of being

Wow. We've covered a lot of ground—well done! In the next chapter, we'll wrap up our work together by reviewing the path you've taken and giving you a glimpse of what living sanely might be like for you. I'll also discuss the paramount importance of being in community with like-minded individuals who understand and support your transformation.

CHAPTER 11

LIVING SANELY IN AN INSANE WORLD

> There are moments when one has to choose between living one's own life
> fully, entirely, completely, or dragging out some false, shallow, degrading
> existence that the world in its hypocrisy demands.
>
> — OSCAR WILDE

Each of us has the equivalent of a Formula 1 race car on our shoulders, yet most people never leave the neighborhood with it, let alone see what it can do on a track. Worse yet, despite driving rather slowly for decades, most people still appear prone to running into curbs, other cars, and even a pedestrian or two from time to time. The unfortunate truth is that most adults have failed to achieve psychological and emotional maturity much beyond that of a teenager. It's no one's fault. We aren't taught how to grow up, let alone realize the benefits of being who we really are in our core. As a result, we suffer and contribute heavily to the suffering of others.

The path of evolution involves two main components: personal emotional responsibility and honesty. Each of us must stop blaming the world and the people in it for our lack of joy and ataraxis. Instead, we must look sincerely and honestly at our internal conditions and transform ourselves by dealing skillfully with what we find.

This book has outlined two paths, developmental and fruitional, that promote such a transformation. We develop the ego function so that it calms down and stops wreaking havoc on our lives and those of others. We must also come to see that the ego function is nothing more than a function that evolved to help us survive. We are so, so much more. The Great Self does not suffer from the small self's core vulnerabilities of insecurity, inadequacy, powerlessness, fragility, and loneliness. It's now your time to be free of them once and for all.

REVIEWING THE PATH WE'VE TAKEN

To understand where we went astray, we started by swimming in a bunch of theory around peace, happiness, and suffering (Chapter 1). You learned that ill-defined goals lead to hopelessly ineffective strategies like circumstance management, aggressive individualism and self-absorption, and emotional suppression and avoidance, which leave us anxious, frustrated, exhausted, stressed out, and possibly even depressed and/or addicted. Complicating matters even further, those strategies inevitably lead to competition and conflict with everyone around us, including those we claim to love. In striving to put all the pieces of the peace-and-happiness puzzle in place, we lose the ability to smell the roses, connect with each other, and find joy, meaning, and purpose in *every* moment.

As Viktor Frankl said, "In the pursuit of happiness, many people fail to find joy." This is the wholly unnecessary tragedy of modern life.

You then learned in Chapter 2 that it all happens the way it does as a direct and inevitable result of misunderstanding who and what we really are and what we're trying to achieve. In Chapter 3, you developed an understanding of our true nature and the immaculate beings that we are. This understanding provides the requisite clarity and sound basis for transformation.

On a closely related note, I've heard many of my family members, friends, and clients wonder what the purpose of life is. I'm going to take a risk and tell you what I've come to believe it may be: *to fully become the real, authentic you and live every moment from that place*. If you refuse to accept this mission, life will find a way (often painfully) to remind you again and again that you aren't doing the work you need to do. That's life's job, and it is very good at it!

I highly suspect you already have some experience with these repeated afflicted patterns; otherwise, you wouldn't have dedicated the time to engage this book and its practices. You have wisely become tired of it, and you're ready for something different.

The antidote, of course, is to be bravely honest and admit that the fundamental challenge you face is that you're living in the wrong way—the way you were taught to live by other confused adults who were also ignorant of their purpose. You are breaking free from the pack, and as your clarity increasingly deepens, you will let your life become an offering, bringing the presence that you are to your work, family, and community. You will be the one who breaks all afflicted cycles. You will stop intergenerational trauma. You will not only transform yourself but will also show others the way forward, thus healing our divided families, social circles, and societies. That, in short, is all I'm doing as a therapist: helping others heal and showing them how to evolve.

It's not about balance. I'm not asking you to add more to-dos to your already overwhelming and impossible-to-achieve to-do list. I'm asking you to integrate mental and emotional transformation into every aspect of your life. You're only ever doing one thing: working skillfully with your mind, heart, and body and directing them toward ever-higher levels of wellbeing. That may seem overwhelming, but that's a misperception because nothing will simplify your life and all the decisions you need to make—both minor and major—once you understand who and what you really are and what you're really doing here on this planet.

The path forward isn't easy. I know that. I am proposing a radical shift in your life by asking you to pry yourself away from the hedonic treadmill—the incessant drive to manage circumstances and distract yourself from the fact that none of it has worked to deliver what you actually want for yourself and your life. If joy and ataraxis are internal conditions requiring cultivation, then you need to get cultivating and never stop. You will know you are doing this when you spend some substantial (but not overwhelming) amount of time formally working on your mind and heart daily.

This radical change in how you conduct your life isn't easy to accomplish, which is why I spent so much time talking about and teaching you how to change your habits in Chapter 4 and cultivate joyful diligence in Chapter 5. Stated simply, all we're ever doing is diligently programming and reprogramming our unconscious minds. There is no such thing as a path of transformation without diligence—the consistent application of skillfulness. And the first thing you must cultivate is the willingness to be uncomfortable in the short term in service to your Great Self's longer-term, higher aspirations. Without such diligence, I'm afraid any project of self-transformation may be over before it has begun, as we often observe with challenging new initiatives like diets and exercise routines.

Start slowly, and allow your new life to grow from a solid base—a clear understanding of who you really want to be (to support the arising of joy and ataraxis), where you're at, and where you want to go—using contemplation.

Once you have cultivated a moderate level of diligence by resolving who you want to be in your mind and heart, it's time to learn *how* to be (Chapter 6). You simply have to get out of your head and into your life. You must stop thinking all the time. I hope you can now see the life-crushing mistake of walking around all day lost in a complicated, judgmental, and afflicted story with you as the self-absorbed central character—a script given to you by confused caregivers living in a confused society. The ego function does nothing but compare the current moment to an ideal moment it imagines is possible (but isn't). It refuses to see that its incessant comparisons and associated demands are the main hindrances to joy, given that it's happy only when getting its way. Thus learning how to rest as awareness represents the greatest personal transformation you will ever undertake. It is, as Loch Kelly likes to describe it, the next phase of human evolution.

The main reason I first taught you *how to be* was so that you would take the rest of the path less personally and experience transformation less arduously. Mastering your emotions (Chapter 7) is impossible while your small self takes them so seriously due to misplaced identification and fears powerful emotions as a result.

They're just emotions! Growing up by developing the ego function with ABCDE practice (Chapter 8) can also seem arduous when you take the perspective that you are the small self with its traumas and all the defensive modes and mechanisms it developed to survive. Those afflicted patterns aren't you, and I've taught you to see through them by seeing what they truly are: a direct and inevitable result of what happened to you and *nothing* more.

Next, you cultivate joy and ataraxis by taking control of karma through ethical thought, speech, and action, which you also accomplish using developmental and fruitional methods. Using the developmental approach, you break karmic loops by reacting more skillfully to the painful situations that arise and the emotions they engender. In short, you live intentionally, and that requires setting intentions and nurturing reflection (Chapter 9) daily. Using the fruitional approach, you learn to transcend the craving for pleasure and aversion to pain by seeing through them when you learn to rest as pure, nondual, nonconceptual awareness (again, Chapter 6). In so doing, you take everything—most notably yourself—less seriously, which provides space for new ways of being. This is what truly allows for stable peace of mind to arise.

Lastly, you must integrate the insights and new perspectives from those more "formal" practices into your life by checking and renewing (Chapter 10) throughout each day. You must break up the mind's neuroticism all day, every day, through intentional redirection. My teacher, Erik Pema Kunsang, has said he wants to become famous for saying that you must do this at least several hundred times a day. While he's certainly kidding about wanting to become famous, he isn't at all kidding about what change requires. You must be vigilant, because your small self is like a child playing with matches who will burn the house down when left unsupervised by the Great Self.

Your Great Self is not a better version of your ego function. It's what's left when the story-based noise, fear, craving, and aversion fall away. It is what's always been quietly watching, knowing, and loving from the background. Thus I've outlined a complete path to bringing this Great Self from the background to the foreground, summarized below.

1. Educate yourself on what joy and ataraxis are and how they are achieved. (Chapters 1 through 3)

2. Learn to break your afflicted habits and establish healthier ones by cultivating joyful diligence. (Chapters 4 and 5)

3. Learn to rest your mind in its true nature as a holder of awareness and realize the Great Self by turning control of the entire system over to that awareness. (Chapter 6)

4. Master your emotions so they stop enslaving you and controlling your thoughts, speech, and actions. This supports nondual awareness practice, because it is the afflictive emotions that powerfully pull a mind back into its primary protective mechanism—the ego function. (Chapter 7)

5. Develop your ego function and mental consciousness so that they stop being in total control of the system and tainting every moment of your life. (Chapter 8)

6. Lead an increasingly intentional, ethical, disciplined, and diligent life; reflect on how it's going; and make the required adjustments. (Chapter 9)

7. Reset your mind throughout the day, driving it toward ever-higher levels of wellness. (Chapter 10)

You will be doing some combination of all these practices for the rest of your life. But the path need not be arduous, because you will increasingly live in the pride and joy of being you—the real you. You will rest knowing that you are no longer a part of the problems on planet Earth; you are *the solution* made manifest.

UNDERSTANDING THE IMPORTANCE OF COMMUNITY

The work you will be doing will lead to your maturation into a very healthy person. Being a grown-up in this world isn't easy, but not because of jobs, bills, taxes, mortgages, and parenting responsibilities. Those things become rather straightforward once you actually grow up and start caring about the right things and prioritizing accordingly. It's more because there aren't many grown-ups around. Clients have asked me about the risk of ending up arrogant or self-righteous. My answer is always the same: Would you feel smug about winning a race against five-year-olds? It won't take much of this work to accelerate away from the pack. While most of that will feel amazing, it can also be difficult because you will quickly find yourself alone.

At that point, my advice for everyone is the same: Get better friends. Just as adults don't develop deep friendships with children who aren't under their care, healthy people don't spend much time with unhealthy people. I have to tell every client struggling in bad friendships and repeated conflicted intimate relationships the same news: When you operate from old wounds and confusion, you attract relationships that reinforce them. As you heal, you will naturally gravitate toward people who support your evolution, and they, in turn, will gravitate toward you. In short, people on the path are simply incompatible with those who just don't get it (yet), and I have yet to witness a transformational path that doesn't include changes to one's social circle.

Your path forward will be challenging, so you'll need to be supported by people who understand and resonate with who you're trying to become (the holder of awareness that you are), what you're trying to accomplish (full realization of your true nature), and how you're living your life as a result (examined, disciplined, and diligent). Thus evolvers need to find, spend quality time with, befriend, and date each other. As you join the community of those working toward authentic wellbeing, you'll be happily pulled along by those who are ahead of you and joyfully help others who are a bit behind you in the process. This is the primary reason I wrote this book: to bring you along with me, because I love you and want you to stop suffering.

So don't despair, but do find the right people to be around. You know where they are because you know what they spend their time doing—exercising, meditating, and attending workshops and retreats like the ones I offer. The more time you spend with people who maintain similar worldviews and life objectives, the easier your path will be. I promise. So please do not discount or neglect the need for community. We grow and heal together because it's the only way forward.

AWAKENING WHAT WAS NEVER LOST

Joy and ataraxis are your birthright as a human being, but you need to cultivate their presence in your mind, heart, and life. They don't often arise on their own. All you're doing with the knowledge and practices in this book is (finally) coming to take what's been yours all along.

I hope you can see that it's more about undoing than doing. No matter who you are or what you've done due to your confusion, you deserve to be happy and peaceful and enjoy deep and fulfilling relationships. You must know this in your core, love. You must also know that the states and traits of mind you desire will inevitably arise if you do the work. Proceed with confidence!

Please hear me with the compassionate but impactful tone I intend. I've tried to wake you from your slumber. With love, clarity, and urgency, I invite you to stop avoiding what you now know in your heart you need to do to have everything you ever wanted.

I will end by succinctly conveying the entire message of this book in one straightforward directive that I hope you will take to heart, delivered in the fun but no-nonsense way I'm increasingly known for: Cut the shit already, and do your work.

AFTERWORD

THE MOST BEAUTIFUL PLATITUDE

> Love is all there is.
>
> — ME (I JUST SAID THAT...LOL)

This book is my tough-love letter to a world I once (inaccurately) believed hurt me deeply. While the picture appears pretty dismal as of 2025, it's also filled with what I understand to be the truest form of hope there is—the knowledge of and confidence in the fact that our suffering will end. I know this because suffering has the cause of confusion and the solution of wisdom. Thus there is only one problem on planet Earth: confusion. The only question is how much suffering we must collectively endure—and how close to the brink we must come—before we accept personal responsibility and make a move.

I know the world is a mess, and I know you know that too. It's easy to become cynical; it's a battle I wage every day. But I also try to remind myself that things are changing because that's all they do, and if we can each bring some genuine intention to our lives to be a little better every day, things will get better...because they have to.

Author L.R. Knost said:

> Do not be dismayed by the brokenness of the world. All things break, and all things can be mended. So go. Love intentionally, extravagantly, unconditionally. The broken world waits in darkness for the light that is you.

Are you willing to open to the possibility that when all is said and done, you will find that the entire purpose of life is to learn how to love? Are you willing to join me in opening to the possibility that you're made of love, light, and wisdom, and to work toward increasingly being those things in the world? Let's run the experiment together and see what happens if we do!

The tide is turning. We can do this in one generation, my friend! I *know* we can get this done, because awakening can be viewed as a technology. It's something we can choose to adopt to make life much easier. Accordingly, it will follow the same bell-curve-looking adoption profile as most every other technology.

Don't be foolish and unwise. Be an early adopter. You have everything you need, so just get it done.

I'd like to close with an instructional poem. Now let me assure you, I know poets, and I don't count myself among them. It just feels like the best way to say what I want to say to close out my initial salvo aimed at the heart of suffering in the West.

The Most Beautiful Platitude

The real you is inherently and innately beautiful beyond description.
The quality of your life in every moment is determined by the quality of your mind.
We will get through this, but you have to do your part.
So please make a move.
Start small, and expand slowly and patiently.
Be diligent, and never be distracted from your mission.
Never fall into despair, hopelessness, or helplessness.
When you falter, as Sam says, begin again.
Begin again.
Begin again.
I am with you always.
I love you. I. LOVE. YOU.
That said, there's no I and no YOU, and there never was.
There's only love. LOVE is all there is and ever was.
Which comes as no surprise to anyone paying attention.
Please pay attention, Love.

APPENDIX I

MALADAPTIVE SCHEMAS

Schemas are an important component of the ABCDE practice outlined in Chapter 8. A schema is a deep mental filter—a core belief or emotional pattern your mind uses to make sense of yourself, other people, and the world. Maladaptive schemas are usually formed in childhood (as a result of traumas) and shape how you think, feel, and react, often without you realizing it. They are nasty little buggers, because they profoundly affect your mental system's predictive priors, attentional control/bias, and subsequent reactions. That means your brain will not only warp its fabrication of reality to fit the schema or otherwise make it true, it will also seek out and focus on *anything* that remotely resembles the schema and then freak out (trigger or hijack) whenever it believes it's found what it's looking for.

I read a story once of someone giving a presentation during a competition. Suffering from a failure schema, he noticed people rolling their eyes, falling asleep, and generally not paying much attention as he presented his work. Even the judges seemed disinterested. Wholly convinced he was failing miserably, he desperately wanted to walk off the stage…and nearly did! But it's a good thing he didn't, because then he wouldn't have won.

This is how schemas keep themselves "true." In therapy, I've observed entire marriages, careers, and lives unnecessarily destroyed by schemas.

Psychologists have outlined 18 to 20 maladaptive schemas, depending on how they're assessed and categorized. Listed below are the original 18 from Dr. Jeffrey Young's book *Schema Therapy*. I describe them according to the ego function and associated core vulnerability, slightly different from the descriptions you may find in other sources.

Abandonment: This is the first of two schemas that seem to represent a more extreme version of the Emotional Deprivation schema (see below). The small self believes that not only will others fail to meet their needs, they will do so intentionally, which represents an abandonment. This confirms feelings of *aloneness* and even *inadequacy/unworthiness*.

Approval and Recognition-Seeking: The small self feels inadequate and, as such, excessively seeks approval, recognition, or even just attention from others, which can present as flamboyance and arrogance. The need for approval can be so strong that this person is willing to change in substantive ways to meet others' expectations and get their attention.

Defectiveness/Shame: The small self feels *inadequate* and *powerless* and believes it is defective, inferior, unlovable, and/or shameful. This can arise as *impostor syndrome*—the feeling that one does not deserve to be in a certain position—accompanied by incessant comparison, hypersensitivity to outcomes or criticisms, and lots of blaming (projection defense).

Dependence/Incompetence: Being *insecure*, *powerless*, and *inade-*

quate, the small self believes it cannot handle life competently and frequently needs help navigating situations. More often than not, this arises as anxiety that can only be assuaged by another.

Emotional Deprivation: The small self sees itself as emotionally *fragile*, *insecure*, and *powerless*, relying on external support for nurturance, empathy, and protection. When these needs go unmet, it interprets the lack of support as confirmation of its isolation and powerlessness, often blaming its own perceived inadequacy or unworthiness. The flawed logic is that its needs would be met if it had value.

Emotional Inhibition: The small self feels *fragile* and *powerless*, so it believes emotions are unsafe to experience because it feels unable to control them. This feeling carries over to others (especially caregivers), assuming that person will also be unable to handle the emotions if expressed, so it inhibits both their experience and expression, respectively. This fear can be around specific categories of emotions such as anger or sadness, or it can apply equally to negative and positive emotions.

Enmeshment/Underdeveloped Self: In an attempt to feel less *alone*, *fragile/insecure*, *powerless*, and *inadequate*, the small self seeks emotional and psychological enmeshment with another person, even when doing so feels suffocating. Enmeshed individuals often lack an entirely separate identity. Enmeshed relationships can feel amazing and *appear* to function quite well, as long as neither party matures into an adult, which is why they usually fail.

Entitlement/Grandiosity: Intensely fearful of *inadequacy*, the small self instead compensates by believing that it is superior and, therefore, entitled to certain rights and privileges others don't deserve. These folks often seek to control inferior others and believe that certain rules should not apply to them, given their superior status.

Failure: Being *inadequate* and *powerless*, the small self is terrified of the inevitable failures to come, which will prove it is deficient and inferior relative to peers. This schema often presents as being hyper-focused on achievement and success in arenas like school, sports, or work, which is a defense mechanism calculated to mask its perception of underlying inferiority. It can also present as an unwillingness to try difficult things. Though similar to the schema of Defectiveness/Shame, this schema focuses on more traditional, objective markers of "success" rather than the more subjective markers of social standing (or lack thereof) within particular groups.

Insufficient Self-Control and Self-Discipline: Being a helpless victim of *fragility* and *powerlessness*, the small self displays a pervasive inability to exercise self-control and restrict emotional impulses, even when failing to do so is likely to result in negative consequences. Immediate gratification is paramount to all other considerations. I've observed in several clients that this can even manifest as a sort of "ADHD light" condition, where a person who is otherwise capable of focus and discipline becomes unable to control their focus when it comes to a task they perceive as even moderately unpleasant.

Mistrust/Abuse: This is the second schema that seems to represent a more extreme version of the Emotional Deprivation schema. The small self believes that not only are others not going to meet their needs, they're also going to intentionally harm it, and being largely *powerless*, the small self will be unable to prevent it.

Negativity/Pessimism: This schema feels like a surrender in that the small self has become hyper-focused on the negative aspects of life experiences while simultaneously discounting or otherwise ignoring the positive aspects. Thus it surrenders to what it perceives as inevitable disappointment. This often presents as a fear of making mistakes or highly elevated expectations that guarantee the schema is frequently confirmed.

Punitiveness: The small self likely feels intense hatred of its own and others' inadequacy and powerlessness, so it exerts control over itself and others through harsh punishment. These folks often feel entitled or grandiose and present as angry, punitive, demeaning, and generally intolerant of others' behaviors, even when such intolerance is hypocritical.

Self-Sacrifice: Being *alone* and *fragile*, the small self voluntarily meets the perceived needs of others by sacrificing its own needs, desires, or emotions. These folks can be highly empathetic—a strength when harnessed skillfully. In this case, however, their empathy is often misplaced/misdirected, shifting the focus of suffering away from itself to become the helper instead of the vulnerable target. These folks pride themselves on being unselfish; however, their perceived unselfishness is often based on unperceived self-absorption, which is why their sacrifices often come with strings attached, like a demand for appreciation.

Social Isolation/Alienation: Having too many experiences that confirmed its *aloneness* and *inadequacy* through exclusion, rejection, or ostracization, the small self becomes genuinely convinced that it is alone in the world and unworthy of being included in a stable tribe, family, group, or community. This leaves them feeling hopelessly isolated and alienated.

Subjugation/Invalidation: The small self feels *inadequate* and is terrified of being *alone*, so it excessively surrenders control out of fear of consequences or of being a burden to others. In doing so, the small self allows its needs to be suppressed or unmet in the service of what it perceives as higher-level priorities, such as acceptance or inclusion.

Unrelenting Standards/Hyper-Criticalness: Intensely fearing *inadequacy*, the small self strives incessantly to meet high standards that are unrealistic at best. These are the hard chargers who sacrifice pleasure, health, and wellbeing in service to the drive, often experiencing perfectionism, rigidity in thinking and rules, and a hyper-focus on efficiency and efficacy.

Vulnerability to Harm or Illness: Being *fragile/insecure* and *powerless*, the small self believes that it is always on the precipice of some kind of emotional, physical, or psychological tragedy.

APPENDIX II

MALADAPTIVE SCHEMA MODES

Because you inadvertently clicked on, downloaded, and installed the schema malware detailed in Appendix I, your brain had to figure out how to navigate, stay safe, and hopefully thrive within the reality defined by the schema virus. To do that, it unconsciously developed maladaptive schema modes, which are patterns of belief, thought, speech, and action that help defend against a core vulnerability and all the resultant feelings. You can consider trauma as the cause of a schema and the schema as the cause of the mode that arose (to defend against the schema). They can be classified according to the standard ways our brains react to traumatizing situations and the emotions generated by them: fight, flight, and freeze.

Schema modes are an important component of the ABCDE practice outlined in Chapter 8. As shown in that chapter's example, the Perfectionist/Overcompensator mode became such an ingrained part of my identity, I'm still occasionally dealing with its harshly critical voice. It arose in response to a Defectiveness/Shame schema—a form of extreme self-doubt. I hope the fact that I'm still dealing with this schema and mode combination isn't discouraging, because it doesn't arise so powerfully and has little to no effect on my life. I see the beauty of it now. A part of my ego function wants to be seen as good, but it doubts itself. Sometimes

I'm gentle with it by trying to let it know it is good and loved. Other times, I just tell it to shut up.

The point is that you will have to determine what "working skillfully with the schemas and modes" means for you.

Innate Child Modes

Angry Child: This reactive mode is bitter, angry, and even vengeful because its core needs for safety, security, connection, and esteem are not being met by the world. The angry child can serve as a protector for the Vulnerable Child (see below) unless and until its anger results in negative consequences such as harsh punishment or rejection/abandonment.

Impulsive/Undisciplined Child: Another reactive mode, the impulsive child feels like a victim and, as such, feels entitled and believes that anything they need to do to alleviate the suffering of the Vulnerable Child (see below) is acceptable regardless of longer-term consequences. They frequently present anger toward anyone who tries to interfere with their pleasure chasing, as if they need to shout at people, "You don't understand, *I'm* the victim here!"

Vulnerable Child: This mode is lonely, sad, vulnerable, inadequate, and insecure and is installed as soon as the mind identifies with the ego function and defines itself as such. This is the "inner child" that pop psychology and many therapists refer to.

Maladaptive Fight Modes

Bully Attacker: This small self defends by lashing out at others or demeaning them to make themselves appear (and feel) superior.

Perfectionist/Overcompensator: This small self attempts to be perfect so that others will more likely meet its needs and confirm its value.

Self-Aggrandizer: This small self can't wait to give you their resume and inflates themselves to ensure others know their value.

Suspicious Overcontroller: This small self is very untrusting of others and situations in general and is often a defense against the severe anxiety that results from feeling powerless.

Maladaptive Flight Modes

Angry Protector: This small self displays aggression to keep troublesome people out of its territory.

Avoidant Protector: This small self avoids situations and people that may trigger distress that exceeds its perceived capabilities.

Complaining Protector: This small self blames everyone and everything else to avoid feeling its vulnerabilities; complaining may also provide some semblance of control over others.

Detached Protector: This small self suppresses feelings and thoughts that are threatening. Note that this is *psychological* avoidance, as opposed to the behavioral/situational avoidance of the Avoidant Protector.

Detached Self-Soother: This small self soothes itself by detaching from feelings by whatever means necessary, often via addictions of myriad varieties: incessant thinking, doomscrolling, media consumption, drugs and alcohol, sex, and gambling. I see this mode in Western society more than others, especially among younger generations.

Maladaptive Freeze Modes

Compliant Surrenderer: This small self is the people pleaser who eagerly surrenders their will to others in a (usually) unsuccessful attempt at having their needs met by others.

Maladaptive Parent Modes

Demanding/Critical Parent: This small self strives for perfection in all matters and often demands that they and all others achieve lest they be deemed worthless. They can rule with an iron fist and are often highly inflexible (because they're right, of course).

Punitive Parent: This small self likely internalized the blame and punishment they received from others and now regularly unleashes it on themselves, others, or (usually) both. This mode refers to the way in which rules and norms are enforced—through punishment of various sorts.

APPENDIX III

DEFENSE MECHANISMS

We've now arrived at the last stage of schema management. Defense mechanisms are the foot soldiers of the schema modes that arise as maladaptive thoughts and behaviors. You can now see the full sequence that occurs in the mind as a result of a trauma.

Trauma → Schema → Schema Mode → Defense Mechanism

Defense mechanisms are an important component of the ABCDE practice outlined in Chapter 8. It's vital to know them because they are usually the first indication that a schema and a resulting schema mode are operating in any given moment.

For example, when I see myself going to great people-pleasing lengths, I know that my small self's Compliant Surrenderer schema mode is operating. That means I have work to do that day, because schemas must be addressed every time they interfere with one's life!

It's important to note that a defense mechanism is a *thought*, such as *There's no way I could've known that the chip was going to blow up* or a *behavior*, such as avoiding a party where you're likely to see your ex-partner. Beliefs can also serve as defense mechanisms, which complicates matters, given their ability to shape perception.

They stem from deep-seated conscious and unconscious assumptions that convince you you're a small self. The key thing to realize about defense mechanisms is that they protect you in the short term but are maladaptive in the long term for many reasons, not the least of which is that they prevent you from living and experiencing a full human life. Most critically though, they prevent you from fully knowing the truth about yourself and your life. Likewise, they prevent others from knowing the same about you, hindering the ability to connect and bond healthily.

Thought-based defense mechanisms manifest as cognitive distortions, like overgeneralization. For example, saying "You never think about me when making a decision!" reflects this distortion. Cognitive distortions attempt to bend reality into whatever the small self/schema mode needs it to be, often to maintain beliefs or justify feelings and reactions. It can be helpful to search the internet for a list of these if you want to get further into this, but it's not necessary.

Acting Out: Performing an extreme behavior to express thoughts or feelings the person feels incapable of expressing. Instead of saying "I'm angry with you," someone who acts out may throw a book or punch a hole in a wall. When a person acts out, it can serve as a pressure release and often helps the individual feel calmer and peaceful once again. For instance, a child's temper tantrum when they don't get their way with a parent is a form of acting out. Self-injury may also be a form of acting out, expressing in physical pain what one cannot stand to feel emotionally. (Note: There are several other reasons for self-harm besides acting out.)

Assertiveness: The presentation of a person's needs or thoughts in a respectful, direct, and firm manner. Communication styles exist on a continuum, ranging from passive to aggressive, with assertiveness falling neatly in between. People who are passive and communicate accordingly tend to be good listeners, but rarely speak up for themselves or their needs in a relationship. People who are aggressive and communicate aggressively tend to be good leaders, but often at the expense of being able to listen empathetically to others and their ideas and needs. Assertive people strike a balance by speaking up for themselves, expressing their opinions and needs respectfully yet firmly, and actively listening to others.

Avoidance: A behavioral defense in which the person takes actions to avoid a situation or, much more often, the feelings likely to result from that situation. Avoiding a party your ex-lover is attending is one example. Drinking and drug use are also behavioral avoidance mechanisms.

Compartmentalization: A milder form of dissociation occurs when parts of oneself remain disconnected from awareness of other parts. An example might be an honest person who cheats on their income tax return and keeps their two value systems distinct and disintegrated while remaining unconscious of the cognitive dissonance.

Compensation: Psychologically counterbalancing perceived weaknesses by emphasizing strength in other areas. By highlighting and focusing on one's strengths, a person recognizes they cannot be great at everything. For instance, when someone says, "I may not know how to cook, but I can do the dishes perfectly," they're trying to compensate for their lack of cooking skills by emphasizing their cleaning skills. When done appropriately and not in an attempt to overcompensate, compensation can help reinforce a person's self-esteem and self-image.

Denial: The refusal to accept reality or fact, suggesting that a painful event, thought, or feeling doesn't exist. Psychologists consider it one of the most primitive defense mechanisms because it typically emerges during early childhood development. Many people use denial in their everyday lives to avoid dealing with painful feelings or areas of their life they don't wish to admit. For instance, a functioning alcoholic will often simply deny they have a drinking problem, pointing to how well they function in their job and relationships.

Displacement: The redirecting of thoughts, feelings, and impulses directed at one person or object but taken out upon another person or object. People often use displacement when they believe they cannot safely express their feelings. The classic example is the man who gets angry at his boss but can't express his anger for fear of being fired. He instead comes home and kicks the dog or starts an argument with his wife. The man redirects his anger from his boss to his dog or wife.

Dissociation: Occurs when a person is no longer present at the moment, even shifting into another representation of themselves to continue navigating the moment. A person who dissociates often loses track of time or themselves and their usual thought processes and memories. In extreme cases, dissociation can lead to a person believing they have multiple selves (dissociative identity disorder). In this manner, a person who dissociates can "disconnect" from the real world for a time and live in a different world that is not cluttered with unbearable thoughts, feelings, or memories.

Intellectualization: The overemphasis on thinking when confronted with an unacceptable impulse, situation, or behavior without employing emotions to help mediate and place the thoughts into an emotional, human context. Rather than deal with the painful associated emotions, a person might employ intellectualization to distance themselves from the impulse, event, or behavior. For instance, a person who has just been given a terminal medical diagnosis, instead of expressing their sadness and grief, focuses instead on the details of all possible fruitless medical procedures. Conspiratorial thinking also often falls under this category.

Projection: The misattribution of a person's undesired thoughts, feelings, or impulses onto another person who does not have those thoughts, feelings, or impulses. People especially use projection when they view certain thoughts as unacceptable or feel deeply uncomfortable having them. For example, a spouse may be angry at their significant other for not listening when, in fact, it is the angry spouse who does not listen. Projection often results from a lack of insight and acknowledgment of one's motivations and feelings.

Rationalization: Twisting a situation into a different light or offering a different explanation for one's perceptions, speech, or behaviors in the face of reality. For instance, a woman dating a man she adores is suddenly and painfully dumped, so she reframes the situation in her mind and thinks, *No big deal—he was a loser anyway.* Or my all-time personal favorite as a therapist, "I didn't have time to complete my eight minutes of daily therapy homework."

Reaction Formation: The converting of unwanted or dangerous thoughts, feelings, or impulses into their opposites. For instance, a woman who is very angry with her boss and would like to quit her job may instead be overly kind and generous toward her boss and express a desire to keep working there forever. She cannot express the negative emotions of anger and unhappiness with her job and instead becomes overly kind to publicly demonstrate her supposed lack of anger and unhappiness.

Regression: The reversion to an earlier stage of development in the face of unacceptable thoughts or impulses. For example, an adolescent who is overwhelmed with fear, anger, and growing sexual impulses might become clingy and start exhibiting earlier childhood behaviors they have long since overcome, such as bed-wetting. An adult may regress under tremendous stress, refusing to leave their bed or engage in everyday activities.

Repression: The *unconscious* blocking of unacceptable thoughts, feelings, and impulses. The key to repression is that people do it unconsciously, so they often have very little control over it. Repressed memories have been unconsciously blocked from access or view. But because memory is very malleable and ever-changing, it is not like playing back a recording of your life. The video has been filtered and even altered by your life experiences or what you've read or viewed. If you struggle to feel subtle sensations/emotions, it can be due to repression. Therapy would likely help.

Sublimation: Channeling unacceptable impulses, thoughts, and emotions into more acceptable ones. For instance, when a person has sexual impulses they do not want to act on, they may instead focus on rigorous exercise. Refocusing such unacceptable or harmful impulses into productive use helps a person channel energy that otherwise would be lost or used in a manner that might cause the person more anxiety. People can also use humor or fantasy as a way to sublimate. Humor, when used as a defense mechanism, is the channeling of unacceptable impulses or thoughts into a lighthearted story or joke. Humor reduces the intensity of a situation and places a cushion of laughter between the person and the impulses.

When used as a defense mechanism, fantasy is channeling unacceptable or unattainable desires into imagination. For example, imagining one's ultimate career goals can be helpful when one experiences temporary setbacks in academic achievement. Both can help a person look at a situation in a different way or focus on aspects of a problem not previously explored.

Undoing: The attempt to take back an unconscious behavior or thought that is unacceptable or hurtful. For instance, after realizing you just insulted your significant other unintentionally, you might spend the next hour praising their beauty, charm, and intellect. By "undoing" the previous action, the person is attempting to counteract the damage done by the original comment.

GLOSSARY

Throughout this book, I use various words somewhat differently from those you might be familiar with and possibly even from the definitions you might find in a dictionary. So I've provided some of the key definitions below for your reference.

Affliction: A troubled state of mind—like stress, anxiety, sadness, anger, or mental agitation—that feels bad. In this book, *affliction* doesn't just mean pain, but also the inner turmoil that comes from fighting reality, fighting emotions, judging yourself or others, or being caught up in destructive habits. Affliction is the opposite of ease, peace, and clarity. It's what we experience when our relationship to what's happening is based in resistance, fear, or craving.

Ataraxis: A deep, lasting sense of inner peace, calm, and ease—the kind that doesn't depend on things going your way. Ataraxis is what it feels like to be grounded, content, and free from the mind's constant worrying and chasing. It's not just the absence of stress or pain, but also the presence of a steady, quiet joy.

Awareness: The knowing aspect of the mind, the primary level of intelligence. It is likely uncaused and, therefore, the primordial cause of everything. In this book, awareness is the calm, clear space in which all your experiences happen. It's who you are at the deepest level—not the thoughts you think or emotions you feel, but the knowing presence that sees them. While vast and all-pervasive by nature, awareness can also be experienced in a localized way (see Figure 2.2 in Chapter 2).

Consciousness: That which turns physical phenomena into an experience known by awareness. There are six primary types: visual, auditory, olfactory, gustatory, tactile, and mental. Mental consciousness includes thoughts of all kinds, including the other five types of consciousness (you can think using images or sounds, just as you think using words). Buddhism also defines a seventh type called the *afflicted consciousness*, which results from ego function identification. The seventh consciousness is dissolved when resting in awareness.

Happiness: A somewhat complicated term that means something different to everyone. Most people believe happiness results from having their pleasures achieved. As such, I've largely avoided using the term and greatly prefer *joy* instead.

Joy: A *state* or *trait* of mind resulting from a *positive relationship to* what's happening (pleasure and pain), based heavily on a particular perspective and grounded in *ataraxis* (a state of serenity, tranquility, contentedness, peace, and ease). The opposite of suffering, joy is a deep sense of wellbeing that doesn't depend on everything going your way. It's not the same as pleasure—it's more like a quiet, stable inner happiness that comes from being at peace with life as it is. Joy isn't about chasing good feelings or avoiding bad ones. It's a trait of mind you can cultivate by changing your perspective and how you relate to each moment—even the hard ones.

Meta-Awareness: Being aware that you're aware. It's the ability to notice not just what you're experiencing (like a thought or emotion), but also the fact that you're experiencing it. For example, instead of just being lost in anger, meta-awareness is noticing *Oh,* anger is happening right now, I am aware of that, and I am aware that I'm aware of it.* It's like stepping back from the movie of your mind and realizing you're the one watching it, not the character on the screen. This kind of awareness gives you more freedom and choice in how you respond to life.

Mindfulness: The simple act of paying attention to what's happening right now—in your body, your mind, and the world around you—without judging it, fighting it, or spacing out. It's noticing your experience as it is instead of getting lost in thoughts, stories, or distractions. Its achievement represents access to Level 2 mind, known as subtle mind, as outlined in Chapter 6.

Non-Arrogant Pride: A healthy sense of satisfaction or gratitude for who you are and how far you've come without feeling superior to anyone else. It's the feeling of "I'm a good person who is working hard and evolving, and I'm proud of that," but without needing to compare, impress, or inflate yourself. This kind of pride is grounded in one's true nature as awareness, the Great Self, humility, and self-respect—not ego. It is the joy of diligence.

Nonconceptuality: Nonconceptuality means experiencing reality directly, without mentally labeling, analyzing, or explaining it. It's what happens when you're simply aware without thoughts, stories, or filters. In this book, nonconceptuality is a key aspect of nondual awareness—the quiet, open presence underneath all the mental noise.

Nonduality: Literally, it means "not two." It points to the deep truth that we are not separate from the world around us. In ordinary life, we feel like there's a separate "me" inside here (the small self) experiencing a world "out there." Nonduality reveals that this split is an illusion—that there's only one seamless reality, and we're not apart from it. In moments of nondual awareness, the sense of being a separate self fades, and there's just peaceful, open knowing of what is.

Pain: A *state* of mind resulting from the *negative subjective appraisal of* a particular moment of consciousness, reflective of *what's happening*.

Peace of Mind: A somewhat complicated term that means something different to everyone, though most people define it as the absence of affliction. It's an inner stability that isn't so easily shaken by pain, problems, or people. In this book, peace of mind comes from changing your relationship to life, not from trying to control it. That said, I've largely avoided using the term and prefer *ataraxis* instead.

Pleasure: A *state* of mind resulting from the *positive subjective appraisal of* a particular moment of consciousness, reflective of *what's happening*.

Pride (vs. Non-Arrogant Pride): The feeling that comes from believing you're better than others—smarter, more successful, more important, or more "right." It often shows up as superiority, arrogance, or the need to prove yourself. While it can feel good for a moment, pride tends to disconnect us from others and fuels self-absorption. In this book, pride is seen as a subtle form of suffering—a fragile identity that needs constant defending. It blocks growth, openness, and genuine connection.

State of Mind (vs. Trait of Mind): How your mind feels and functions in a given moment. It includes your mood, thoughts, level of energy, and how you're relating to what's happening. For example, being anxious, angry, joyful, calm, or focused are all different states of mind. States come and go; they're temporary and can shift quickly. This book explores how these shifting states are shaped by deeper traits and habits, and how to relate to them skillfully.

Suffering: A *state* or *trait* of mind resulting from a *negative relationship to* what's happening (pleasure and pain), based heavily on a particular perspective and grounded in *affliction* (a state of turmoil, agitation, discontent, anxiety, and stress). The opposite of joy, it's what happens when your mind says, *This shouldn't be happening* and you get stuck in anger, fear, sadness, or stress. Two people can go through the same situation, but only one might suffer, because suffering depends on how you *relate* to what's happening, not just what's happening. Suffering can be eliminated entirely and is not experienced by the Great Self.

Trait of Mind (vs. State of Mind): A long-term pattern in how your mind usually works or reacts—like a mental habit that sticks around over time. Traits of mind include things like being generally anxious, joyful, patient, or reactive. Unlike temporary states of mind, traits are more stable and automatic. In this book, we focus on cultivating positive traits (like equanimity or joy) through repeated practice, so that peace and wellbeing become your default, not just a passing experience.

ENDNOTES

1 Maureen Groppe and Sarah Elbeshbishi, "Exclusive Poll: Overwhelming Majority Says the U.S. Faces a Mental Health Crisis," *USA Today*, last modified January 10, 2022, https://news.yahoo.com/exclusive-poll-overwhelming-majority-says-100020629.html.

2 Lawrence Hamilton, "Conspiracy vs. Science: A Survey of U.S. Public Beliefs," University of New Hampshire Carsey School of Public Policy, last modified April 25, 2022, https://carsey.unh.edu/publication/conspiracy-vs-science-survey-us-public-beliefs.

3 Mattieu Ricard, *Happiness: A Guide to Developing Life's Most Important Skill* (Little, Brown & Company, 2007).

4 Robert Wright, *Why Buddhism Is True: The Science and Philosophy of Meditation and Enlightenment* (Simon & Schuster, 2017).

5 Daniel Goleman and Richard Davidson, *Altered Traits: Science Reveals How Meditation Changes Your Mind, Brain, and Body* (Penguin Random House, 2017).

6 Sam Harris, *Waking Up: A Guide to Spirituality Without Religion* (Simon & Schuster, 2014).

7 Chris Niebauer, *No Self, No Problem: How Neuropsychology Is Catching Up to Buddhism* (Hierophant Publishing, 2019).

8 Sam Harris, *Waking Up: A Guide to Spirituality Without Religion* (Simon & Schuster, 2014).

9 Andrea Zaccaro, Andrea Piarulli, Marco Laurino, Erika Garbella, Danilo Menicucci, Bruno Neri, and Angelo Gemignani, "How Breath-Control Can Change Your Life: A Systematic Review on Psycho-Physiological Correlates of Slow Breathing," *Frontiers in Human Neuroscience* 12,

no. 353. https://www.frontiersin.org/journals/human-neuroscience/articles/10.3389/fnhum.2018.00353/full.

10 Michael Easter, *The Comfort Crisis: Embrace Discomfort to Reclaim Your Wild, Happy, Healthy Self* (Rodale Books, 2021).

11 Thomas Nagel, "What Is It Like to Be a Bat?" *The Philosophical Review* 83 no. 4, 435–450. (1974). https://www.sas.upenn.edu/~cavitch/pdf-library/Nagel_Bat.pdf.

12 M. R. Leary and J. Guadagno, "The Role of Hypo-egoic Self-processes in Optimal Functioning and Subjective Wellbeing." In Kennon M. Sheldon, Todd B. Kashdan, and Michael F. Steger, eds., *Designing Positive Psychology: Taking Stock and Moving Forward* (Oxford University Press, 2011).

13 Jenn Shapland, *Thin Skin: Essays* (Penguin Random House, 2023).

14 Bernardo Kastrup, *Analytic Idealism in a Nutshell: A Straightforward Summary of the 21st Century's Only Plausible Metaphysics* (London: Collective Ink Ltd., 2023).

15 Andy Clark, *The Experience Machine: How Our Minds Predict and Shape Reality* (Pantheon, 2023).

16 "Adelson, Edward H, Ph.D.," Brain and Cognitive Sciences Directory, accessed July 24, 2025, https://bcs.mit.edu/directory/edward-h-adelson.

17 Beata Stahre Wästberg, "How to Convert Reality into Virtual Reality: Exploring Colour Appearance in Digital Models," thesis, February 2009.

18 Ibid.

19 Michael Bicks, Anna Lee Strachan, David Alvarado, and Jason Sussberg, directors, "Your Brain: Perception Deception," *NOVA*, season 50, episode 9, aired May 17, 2023, on PBS; executive producers Julia Cort and Chris Schmidt.

20 Dzigar Kongtrul Rinpoche, *Diligence: The Joyful Endeavor of the Buddhist Path* (Shambhala Publications, 2024).

21 Ibid.

22 Charles Duhigg, *The Power of Habit: Why We Do What We Do in Life and Business* (Random House, 2014).

23 Carol S. Dweck, PhD, *Mindset: The New Psychology of Success* (Ballantine Books, 2008).

24 Bruce Tift, *Already Free: Buddhism Meets Psychotherapy on the Path of Liberation* (Sounds True, 2015).

25 David Goggins, *Can't Hurt Me: Master Your Mind and Defy the Odds* (Lioncrest Publishing, 2018).

26 Rinpoche, *Diligence*.

27 Steve Magness, *Do Hard Things: We Get Resilience Wrong and the Surprising Science of Real Toughness* (HarperCollins, 2022).

28 Rinpoche, *Diligence*.

29 Loch Kelly, *Shift into Freedom: The Science and Practice of Open-Hearted Awareness* (Sounds True, 2015).

30 Daniel Goleman and Richard J. Davidson, *Altered Traits: Science Reveals How Meditation Changes Your Mind, Brain, and Body* (Penguin Random House, 2017).

31 Tift, *Already Free*.

32 Magness, *Do Hard Things*.

33 Jeffrey E. Young, Janet S. Klosko, and Marjorie E. Weishaar. *Schema Therapy: A Practitioner's Guide* (Guilford Press, 2003).

ADDITIONAL RESOURCES

My website
www.UnbreakableInc.com

The Effortless Mindfulness Institute
www.LochKelly.org/effortless-mindfulness-institute

The Essentia Foundation
www.EssentialFoundation.org

The Schema Therapy Society
www.SchemaTherapySociety.org/Schema-Therapy

IN GRATITUDE

My father always said, "To whom much is given, much is expected." I've been given an awful lot, and this effort has been, in part, an attempt to repay a small portion of that debt.

I'd like to thank my teachers and mentors from the West and the East for their patience, knowledge, and wisdom. Any errors, omissions, or misunderstandings herein are the responsibility of this author.

There are more people to thank than I can possibly fathom. First and foremost, this book wouldn't exist without the constant love and support of my dear wife Jami. Thank you for believing in me and taking a wrecking ball to this ego function's chronic self-doubt. Your confidence in me is the rock I stand on every day. Thank you especially for running our household for years while I wrote, rewrote, and rewrote again. You are an unselfish helper to so many every day of your life. Please relax into the goodness you radiate.

My parents, sister, and children also deserve a major callout for their incessant love and support, which I have enjoyed each day of my life. Thank you for showing me what unconditional love is.

To Anna, Bella, and Marshall: I've tried to show you what it means to be a decent, hardworking, happy, peaceful, and especially loving human in this challenging world. Please forgive my failings, and do your best in life.

Speaking of children, much gratitude to my ex-wife Jen for being the best co-parent anyone could ask for. We found a way to get along despite many differences of opinion, and I am proud of our efforts. We did good.

Thank you to my therapy clients, especially those I was unable to help as much as I would've preferred. I will remain in this fight with you until we're all done with this ridiculous, needless suffering.

Much gratitude to Professor Fred Stone, PhD. Your competence inspired me to grow into the therapist I am today. Thank you to JoAnna for guiding me through licensure. I stand on the ethical framework you exemplify. Thank you to Marc for giving me the confidence to practice therapy the only way we know it needs to be done—with Fierce Love. My clients benefit from your bravery and all that you are in the world. Thank you for your sound mentorship.

Thank you to Catherine, Nathan, Sydney, and the rest of the folks at Modern Wisdom Press, and to John Kellow for connecting us. What a difference a day makes. Whatever assistance this book provides is due to your guidance and mentorship. You are the only publisher who heard me.

Much thanks to my dear friend and Vajrayana mentor Gary, who taught me how to write without exhausting my readers. Our friendship has existed for centuries and will never end.

Shoutout to my kalyanamitra Ashley, who also unselfishly assisted the early editing process.

Thank you to Michael for dragging me kicking and screaming

onto the path. I wish you well. Thank you to my teacher Loch Kelly for trusting me to include a few of your wonderful practices in this book.

Much love to my dear teachers Pema Khandro Rinpoche and especially Erik Pema Kunsang and his loving wife Tara, who are the finest examples of angels I may have ever met (as far as I know). Thank you both for restoring my trust in Buddhist teachers, for showing me directly what it means to be a Vajrayana Buddhist in this world, and for exemplifying a relationship based in selfless love and mutual respect.

There are myriad others worthy of thanks and praise. You know who you are. Thank you. My gratitude to you is boundless.

Most of all, thank you to the Buddha and all my Buddhist teachers who saved me from a life of abject suffering. You taught me how to love a world I once despised and enjoy the sheer bliss of being a small part of the solution instead of a big part of the problem.

ABOUT THE AUTHOR

Joseph (Joe) DeNicholas, MBA, LCSW, is a licensed therapist in private practice whose work bridges the worlds of science, spirituality, and healing. He holds a bachelor's degree in electrical engineering, a master's in business, and a master's in social work, bringing a rare interdisciplinary perspective to his clinical and contemplative work. With over two decades of dedicated study in Tibetan Buddhist psychology and advanced training under some of the world's most respected meditation masters, Joe helps individuals access deep transformation, clarity, and peace. He has guided hundreds of people in developing meaningful meditation practices, including many navigating the unique challenges of incarceration.

Before transitioning to a life of service, Joe played various roles supporting the global shift to energy-efficient lighting, earning multiple US patents in integrated circuit and semiconductor device design.

Joe's current focus lies in integrating Buddhist psychology with modern neuroscience and neuropsychology to relieve suffering and unlock the mind's natural capacity for peace, joy, connection, and wellbeing.

He is the founder of Unbreakable Inc., an organization devoted to helping people reconnect with their innate resilience and goodness—often buried beneath layers of trauma, anxiety, and depression. Through a powerful blend of education, meditation, and therapy, Unbreakable Inc. supports people in experiencing themselves and their lives in radically new and liberating ways.

Joe lives in Boulder County, Colorado, with his beloved wife Jami, daughters Anna and Bella, and stepson Marshall. He's an avid lover of astronomy, nature, and sports—and a lifelong learner committed to the path of awakening.

www.ingramcontent.com/pod-product-compliance
Lightning Source LLC
Chambersburg PA
CBHW060517080526
44586CB00012B/514